EXPERIENCING LIFE AS A

YOGI

Youthful Observant Great

ATUL ANAND

PAPER TOWNS
PUBLISHERS

PAPER TOWNS
PUBLISHERS

First published by
Papertowns Publishers
72, Vishwanath Dham Colony,
Niwaru Road, Jhotwara,
Jaipur, 302012

Experiencing Life as a Yogi

ISBN Print Book - 978-93-87131-91-0

Cover Design by Aditi Shah
Instagram Id: @the.book.story
aditicshah01@gmail.com

EXPERIENCING LIFE AS A

YOGI

Youthful Observant Great Individual

TABLE OF CONTENTS

ACKNOWLEDGEMENTS / GRATITUDE

I want to start by expressing my sincere gratitude to "Almighty – GOD – Parmatma" all Gurus for inspiring me to be able to write and complete this book. Sincere thanks to Guru Dev Shri Shri Ravi Shankar Ji for giving the gift of Sudarshan Kriya Yoga to all people around the world. I was able to regain my health back due to regular practice of it.

My thanks for other Gurus – Yogananda, Sadhguru, Gaur Gopal Das, Swami Sarvapriyananda, Brahma Kumaris sister Shivani Ji, Mukesh Agarwal sir, sister Chitra Khandelwal Ji, EV Swami sir, Girish Bhai, Balakishore Ji, Sneh Desai and many more, whose teachings have inspired to me put down my thoughts and interpretation of this vast subject of Yoga and meditation and how we can bring transformation in this world by imbibing these practices at individual, leadership, corporate and social level.

I want to express my deepest thanks to all friends and Mentors in writing. Special thanks to Nitin Agarwal, Ankit Jhamb for guiding me on my journey for the FIRST novel of my life.

I want to express my thanks to family and extended family members in particular – my father – Pawan Pachlangia (for teaching me Yoga and introducing me to the Art of Living family) and mother – Sumitra Devi. Special thanks to my wife – Neha Sharma, my daughter – Anika and my little son – Aadvik, it is because of your support that I was able to complete this book, which is the passion of my life.

I want to express my gratitude to my current and all my earlier organizations and this corporate world since it is my karma bhoomi which is helping me to learn so many new things every day in my corporate life.

I want to thank all my well-wishers (known and unknown) for showering so much of blessings which have helped me to complete this book.

PREFACE

I thought of writing this book to share the journey of my life from the corporate corridors to experiencing life as a YOGI. I certainly consider YOGI as an acronym – Youthful, Observant, Great, Individual soul consciousness. We all are so engrossed in our daily life, at more of "BODY consciousness level". Time has come that we should start realizing our true potential and nature – "Soul consciousness".

During my journey of writing this book – I have researched and experienced – YOGA and MEDITATION as part of my life for more than a decade. As a part of this book, I have myself gone through more than thousands of hours of Yoga and meditation practice. During these practices, I have experienced multiple transformational experiences, and I have finally understood the very purpose of this life. I want to share my knowledge with the wider world to bring the change in the world at a very fundamental level.

I have divided this book majorly in 5 parts – 1st part is my journey from the corporate world to be Yogi, in which I have shared my life experiences of transformation.

In the 2nd part – I have tried putting in all the research and knowledge which I have gathered through years of Yoga practices, attending advance meditation sessions, watching thousands of hours of YouTube videos of my gurus – Sri Sri Ravi Shankar Ji, Sadhguru, Gaur Gopal Das, Swami Sarvapriyananda and Brahma Kumaris. Learnings of all these GURUs pointed out in one direction of life and helped me understand and answer various questions of life.

In the 3rd Part – I have put in an effort to answer some tough questions of Life: WHO AM I, what is GOD, the LAW of KARMA and more. I have tried answering these questions from my own spiritual knowledge that I acquired from attending and practising Yoga and meditations from these masters. The intent of answering these questions is not to hurt anyone's sentiments or viewpoints, but to be as honest as possible. I would be undoubtedly fine if an individual doesn't feel or doesn't agree to these answers of mine and I would completely respect it. Still, I have put my sincere efforts in putting up pearls of wisdom by referring to multiple masters, and these thoughts are not my original contribution. This vast ocean of knowledge was already there. I have just tried compiling it based on my understanding. Please forgive me if there are any mistakes in my compilation of this vast sea of spiritual knowledge.

In the 4th part – I have focused on how we can bring transformation in the world by following these practices. We know that in this digital world – there are multitudes of problems such as Stress being a silent killer, how we as humans can contribute and address to these problems as individuals, leaders at a corporate-level, enterprise-level or in the start-up ecosystem, society and nations at large.

In the 5th part – I have tried sharing few pictures of smiling faces after doing Yoga and meditation session

In this book, I have tried putting my efforts to share my learnings and practices of decade and hours of Yoga and Meditation. I hope you will like it. Keep reading and enjoying my this and other upcoming books.

Some of the diagrams, such as seven layers of existence and three faculties of the soul, are more of the artistic representation for easier understanding and depiction.

PART 1

JOURNEY FROM THE CORPORATE WORLD TO BE A YOGI

> Finding Harmony in Chaos, Bliss in Suffering, Wisdom in Foolishness, Light in Darkness, Immortality in a place of Death is Bhagvad Gita .
>
> – GURU DEV SRI SRI

END OF THE ROAD

Being a Technocrat at heart, 5th Oct 2011, was like a black day for me and I am sure for most of the other tech-enthusiasts since we lost one of the most significant technology ICONS of 21st Century – Steve Jobs.

I got to read about Steve Jobs' final words when his sister – Mona Simpson allowed the New York Times to publish the eulogy she delivered at his memorial service on 16th October.

Steve's final words, hours earlier, were monosyllables, repeated three times.

Before embarking, he'd looked at his sister Patty, then for a long time at his children, then at his life's partner, Laurene, and then over their shoulders past them.

Steve's final words were:

OH WOW. OH WOW. OH WOW.

Mona Simpson is a novelist and a professor of the English language at the University of California, Los Angeles. Since 1988, she has held the Sadie Samuelson Levy Chair in Languages and Literature at Bard College. She delivered this eulogy for her brother, Steve Jobs, on 16th October

2011, at his memorial service at the Memorial Church of Stanford University.[1]

From Steve's last words and last glances, my belief in life got even more firmed up. Emotions and relationships always bond humans. In your last days, you always wish to be surrounded by your loved ones. I had heard about going back to basics several times, but I was never able to understand the fundamental meaning of this, till the day when I thought that it was almost the end of the road for me as well, while I was thinking about my tech ICON – Steve Jobs.

It was an ordinary life of the IT professional handling escalations and system issues, and I only thought of Systems as IT systems, servers, big box, racks, memory blades – my thinking was so constrained. Then that black night came which had brought the dawn of new life for me.

I got a call at 1:00 a.m. I was almost sleeping at that time. I picked up the phone and answered it without seeing who is there on the other side. I heard the voice of my colleague saying, "Hey, wake up! wake up!"

He sounded as if he was alarming me of my life coming to an end in the next few seconds. I asked him what has happened. His voice was still cracking as he told me about how our ERP systems were down for the last 30 mins. He had an initial discussion with the vendor, and they were trying to find the cause of the issue which would take another half an hour. That half-hour stretched into an ordeal of 48+ hours before the problem was detected correctly, and we arrived at a logical conclusion.

It was hours of phone calls with more than 100+ people on the phone trying to investigate what went wrong. There was so much of panic, unclarity and confusion all around. I still remember it

---

1 https://www.nytimes.com/2011/10/30/opinion/mona-simpsons-eulogy-for-steve-jobs.html?pagewanted=all

was more noise and less fruitful discussion, and with each passing hour, the intensity of that noise kept increasing. Suddenly one site engineer came and told it was an issue with basic switch failure in datacenter resulting in this whole issue.

Then I understood the meaning of "going back to basics for solving the issue" in the professional world.

Although the issue was resolved with minor damage to the ERP system and the business, I did observe that this 48+ hours of non-stop damage control had done severe damage to me from the inside and the signs of this damage started showing up in me with numbness in legs, severe pain and irritation. When I woke up the next morning, my lower back was in extreme pain. I was not able to get up from the bed myself and had to ask my wife for help. At first, I blamed myself for my bad posture and not sleeping properly during the night. However, I later realized that the issue was more severe and fundamental in nature. It was now time for me to discover the meaning of "going back to basics" in my personal life. I knew deep inside that this was something more serious. We somehow managed that day; I took a day off from my office, and rested the whole day on my bed, hoping that the pain would subside and the situation would improve. A couple of days passed by and the intensity of pain didn't lower, so we finally decided to visit an orthopaedic. He gave me some pain killers and antibiotics for my symptoms. Still, I was aware that it wouldn't be able to provide me with any long-term relief. I even visited a couple of physiotherapists; there was a time when it appeared to me as if I was wasting my hard-earned money without being adequately treated for the pain.

Moreover, the pain was irregular, so it was impacting my professional career as well. I wondered if I would ever be able to play freely with my 1-year-old daughter then, or would I ever be able to hold her in my arms. It was quite a tough time for me personally, and I started accepting pain as the way of my life.

It was in March that we planned to visit our hometown Jaipur for our annual vacation. Being a goody boy at home, I was welcomed warmly by my parents. As part of the usual joint family practice, my father got to know about me suffering from back pain from my mother. He came and told me, "My boy, you are ageing now!" That remark from my father raised the alarm in my mind – Was I getting that old? My whole life, since childhood, passed by me in a flash of a few seconds. I realized that till now, I was all busy with running around for studies and earning my basic needs. But what would happen if my body would not be well for enjoying those needs? Something in me changed that day– it was a time for a self-check and realization. I made a promise to myself to not have a miserable life any longer. I would once again take back control of my life.

My father, who was then serving in the bank, was a regular Yoga practitioner. I had always seen him doing Asanas and Pranayama for at least an hour every day. He always made this statement, 'You invest 60 mins a day on yourself in the form of Yoga or exercise, and you would get three times the benefit'. He introduced me to some asanas, pranayamas and kriyas for healing my body. I started it with reluctance and disbelief every day. Still, a part of me kept telling myself that it had already begun working positively in terms of reducing my pain and controlling it all together. I started devoting almost an hour daily on myself. I used to work on my body and mind to prepare it for handling the rest of my eventful day.

The initial 90 days were the most challenging days of my life; since every day, I made this habit for sparing 60 mins on my body, mind and soul and it worked, and magic started happening in front of my eyes. I was in better control of myself physically and emotionally.

I got so much used to Yoga that I always used to wake up early in the morning. I still remember my first day when I did Kriya Yoga. I was able to feel the energy flow in my body for the first time. I was able to feel the healing of my backbone pain. I was able to see the flexibility in my body.

There are three major drivers which make the person do something in life

Love – If you love something passionately, then you would do the stuff without thinking much about it

Greed – Greed is another primary driver which propels an individual for performing any actions. Greed is such a powerful force that it drives individuals, organizations, economies, nations and the whole world. There are many stories in history and recent past where the real driving force was greed

Fear – fear always works when love and greed fail to drive any actions. Fear lays deep in our subconscious mind. The fear of losing something precious in life always keeps you going.

In my case, the factor of fear was the initial driver for me to start taking care of my body; the fear of being unable to hold my daughter up in my arms, and the fear of being permanently bed-ridden. Later I started enjoying Yoga as it became an indispensable part of my schedule. Since then, I have felt the love for Yoga in my life. I think Yoga is so much synonymous to my personality that it became my priority in life, and it worked for me.

FORMAL INTRODUCTION OF YOGA IN MY LIFE

It was during my initial sessions on acquiring knowledge of Yoga. We were there in 6 days session on Yoga and Meditation in the vast basement in a Yoga Camp. We were more than 20 people who had enrolled in this program, and I found myself surprisingly the youngest of all in terms of age, but I knew that I was undergoing severe lower back pain. I knew that I was not even able to stand up for the basic warm-up exercise for 10 mins. That situation showed me my real mirror in terms of my state of health. It was like an eye-opener for me. I also observed one person who had to be carried down through the staircase by a couple of people. This person was offered a chair to sit since he was not able to sit on the floor. As a part of getting to know each other, we all introduced ourselves in different manners. He just told his name and said that he was suffering from cancer and had only a few months left. He said he wanted to die since he could not bear the pain. I immediately understood the back pain, which I was suffering, was nothing in comparison to his pain. All the participants froze for a few seconds after knowing this. He was in his early 40's in terms of age; he was a very lean, thin guy, almost like a skeleton. I was not able to digest that thought that at such a young age, this man had turned into a skeleton due to the most incurable disease on the earth.

Although our Yoga Guru knew that fact and he gave a generous look at the person, and Guruji started the session with a big smile. We were introduced with different processes and techniques every day, and in the concluding remarks, our Yoga guru would give us some homework to do at home and then he would discuss the homework and revise those concepts and told the new processes and concepts. I was keeping track of that person regularly. I was seeing visible improvements and changes in him. On the first day, he was very restricted in his movements in performing Yoga processes. Next day, I was able to see the smile on his face for the first time, and he was participating in all the functions. On the last day of the session, he was quite excited and got a new reason for living his life. In the concluding comments, we all had to share our experiences. He told me that he wanted to live life for a longer time with all happiness around him in this situation. I saw the visible transformation in a cancer suffering person in just six days. It was one of the most phenomenal and memorable experiences of life which I had.

3 MINS CHALLENGE STORY

I remember a small incident in my past organization wherein we were celebrating the health awareness week and a doctor from a reputed hospital came up for delivering a lecture on the importance of health in our life and treating it as our priority. During that small span of 10 mins, I was able to rewind my whole story of back pain, which I had undergone in my past few years and how I had recovered from it. I consider it was apparent for me to experience and correlate to every word of what the doctor was mentioning since it was a distant memory of fear and pain. The next thing that happened to me in my life was such a eureka moment that I hadn't anticipated. Doctor asked for ten volunteers from the audience for participating in a challenge, and I saw there were 9 of them going on the stage, and I was in a dilemma whether I should go or not. What would the challenge be like? Would I be able to do it or not? But someone from the audience called out my name, and I had to go on the stage to avoid any embarrassment for calling out my name again. The doctor asked us to take positions for the challenge – It was a 3 mins plank challenge. We were getting ready for the challenge, and here came the whistle sound for starting of the challenge.

We all started the challenge. We heard the cheering sound coming from the hall. Everyone was cheering us up for going ahead "Go On…Go On…." And suddenly we saw participants dropping out of the plank posture due to pain, and the count for drop-outs was increasing from one-two to as high as seven. After the end of two minutes, only three people were left, including me. Another 10 seconds and another person dropped down. So, at two mins and twenty seconds, only me and one more person. It was now two mins and 30 seconds, and everyone was cheering for us. As we were about to complete the 2 mins 40 seconds mark, that other person also gave up. It was just a matter of another twenty more seconds. It was me alone now. The stopwatch signalled the completion of 3 minutes. I was still rock solid. I saw people clapping for me, and they told me to come out of this plank position already; the challenge was over. Somehow, I was still holding it on, and finally, judges told me to leave the plank position. It was a victorious moment for me. I retrospected my last 5 mins there and then, from being hesitant to participate in the 3 mins plank challenge to emerging as the winner of the same. When I started, I was not even confident of completing it in the first place, but here I emerged victorious for the same.

That was the first time I re-experienced the magic happening in my body. From the painful backbone couple of years ago, that day, I was able to hold the plank position for more than three minutes. Something in me was changing, and I was not even aware of that inner strength which was developing in me.

THE BANGKOK STORY

A few months later, our IT leadership team and I were travelling to Bangkok for some offsite workshop. It was a jam-packed schedule for a three days session. Just after reaching Bangkok, I had twisted my left ankle and was in severe unbearable pain. I was supposed to deliver a Yoga session for my team members from different nationalities in the Asia Pacific very early the next morning. I was worried whether I would be able to walk by myself. On the following day early morning, I walked down to the Yoga session hall and conducted the session of one and a half hours without much pain. Individuals who were aware of my twisted ankle came up to me after completion of the session, asking me about my wellbeing and with a big smile on my face, I gave them the reply.

We had our regular planned sessions during the three days' time. On the concluding day of the workshop, everyone was asked to write one adjective for each other on the "Wall of Gratitude", and I was surprised to see my colleagues writing words like – Teacher,

Yogi, instructor, master for me. It was such an emotional and humbling moment for me to see such warm feelings from my colleagues. This was again a testimony for me that I was getting transformed from being a mere IT professional to a person with a more profound sense of responsibility and gratitude towards individuals. All my colleagues started respecting me more, not because of my professional knowledge but for having more human-centric values.

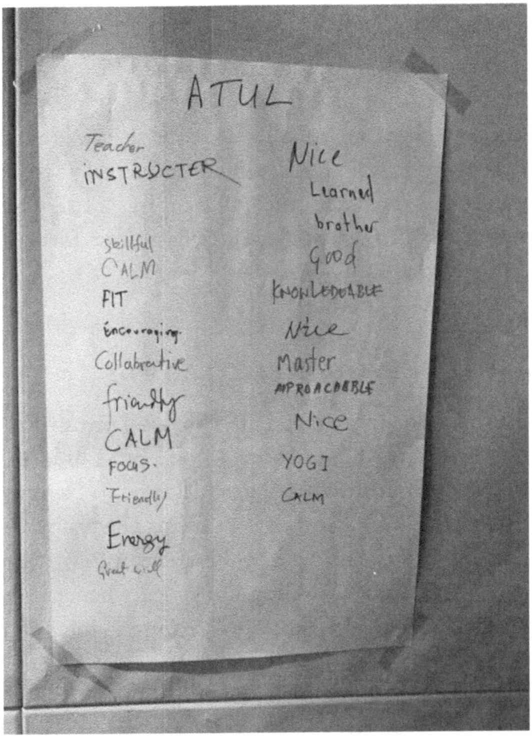

Whenever I share my Bangkok story with my childhood and college friends – they all start laughing at me, saying that after going to Bangkok, what you did or taught was "Yoga" to others and they gave me a nickname – Yogi, which I started liking.

We had this International Yoga week celebrations planned in our office, and I was privileged to take sessions for my office colleagues. I was asked to give a short speech on Yoga during one of our weekly stand-up call in front of 250+ company colleagues. I felt the same way Swami Vivekananda would have felt more than a century back on 11th September 1893 when he had graciously addressed the parliament of religions in Chicago. I remembered him briefly for a few seconds and started with my speech on Yoga. Swamiji's passion for the discourse on Hinduism was genuinely marvellous, and I always consider Swami Vivekananda as my ideal. I felt proud that what I started practising at home for myself was now more of the passion for me to teach others as well, and to my surprise, it was appreciated by my colleagues as well. I got to explore the real passion within me. I understood what kept me going on was a real passion for contributing back to the society in whatsoever form of skills which I possess.

FROM JUST BEING A PAPA TO A YOGI

I want to share one more incident, which is a great memory for me to cherish. When I used to be a small kid, I used to see my father doing Yoga in front of me, and I used to have very little interest during my childhood days. It seems like history repeated itself after 30 odd years but in quite a surprising and pleasant way. I used to do Yoga in early mornings when my daughter used to be still asleep. One fine Sunday, my daughter and I both woke up a bit late, and she knew that papa would do Yoga as part of his daily routine. She told me something in my ears before I started with my regular Yoga. Just to let you all know, my daughter had lots of dolls, teddy bears, dollhouses and other soft toys. She brought all those soft toys on the bed close to me. They were more than 40 in number. She made sure all those soft toys, and dolls had a proper place on the bed. I was still surprised and scratching my head about what my daughter was after. I was thinking that she and her mom had plotted something against me to avoid me from doing my daily Yoga chorus. She told me, papa, I got to know that you had performed Yoga in Thailand, Bangkok, with so many different nationalities. Could be please perform Yoga for my soft toys, dolls and teddy bears. They wanted to see your Yoga for a long time, and they had told me this in my dreams. I was surprised at first and got so humbled by my daughter saying these words, that her dollhouse and soft toys wanted to see my Yoga. I had a celebrity feeling and fulfilment from inside. She told me that this bed is like a stadium. I had bought all the tickets for my dolls, soft toys to watch your Yoga exclusively and she made a statement that papa please don't be nervous with such a stadium full of audience, I know that you will not be scared. Still, I just thought of saying, please give your best in front of my audience. I smiled back at her and started performing my Yoga routines. It took me almost an hour, and she was closely following all my Yoga moves and stretches, and I asked my little daughter – Did you and your audiences liked it and were it a value for money for you? She hugged me and told me that the best thing which I like about you papa is your Yoga and you are a true Yogi. Those words from my daughter made my day and still echoes in my ears whenever I feel low and down during my routine corporate life.

I had taken multiple Yoga sessions with 100's of individuals around the world in my life, but still, this incident is the most memorable and precious one in my life.

PART 2

QUEST FOR KNOWLEDGE

> There are two mistakes one can make along the road to truth: not going all the way, and not starting.
>
> – Gautam Buddha

INTERNATIONAL DAY OF YOGA[2]

International Yoga day is celebrated across the world on 21st June. There is a significance of choosing 21st June since it is the longest day of the year in the northern hemisphere, considered as the summer solstice. While addressing the 69th session of United Nations General Assembly on 27TH SEPTEMBER, 2014 Prime minister of India – Shri Narendra Modi urged the world on the importance of Yoga and to adopt International Day of Yoga. On 11th December 2014, 193 members UN General Assembly approved the proposal with record 177 countries supporting the resolution for adopting 21st June as the international day for Yoga. The 1st International Day of Yoga was organized on 21st June 2015 by the Ministry of AYUSH at Rajpath, New Delhi. A couple of world records were created on 1st International day of Yoga since a maximum number of participants from different countries contributed to the Yoga session. It is one of the proud moments for India, wherein we have contributed to creating a healthy world.

---

2 International Day of Yoga – Common Yoga Protocol – Government of India

YOGA BACKGROUND STORY- HISTORY

We, as human beings, are always good storytellers. As part of my initial research on the origins of "yoga", I had read many literature books and articles. I heard more than hundreds of hours of videos, many stories were being told, but this particular one best suited my logical mind regarding the origin of "yoga". Hence, I thought of telling this short story of how Yoga was propagated on this earth. The origin of Yoga could be traced back thousands of years in the history of human existence. It was believed that Lord Shiva is the Adi-guru who had first taught this to the seven sages called "Saptrishis.

Lord Shiva was sitting and meditating in silence on the banks of lake Kantisarovar for quite some time. Then people gathered around him in curiosity to know what was happening. Suddenly hundreds of people were around him, thinking Lord Shiva would open his eyes and share some spiritual insights. After a few months of waiting, slowly and gradually, people started leaving from that place since lord Shiva was sitting rock-solid in his meditation and didn't open his eyes. In the end, only seven sages stayed back till the end when Lord Shiva opened his eyes to impart these seven sages the fundamental knowledge of Yoga. Sage – Agastya who was the most popular for propagating Yoga to the Indian subcontinent. Hundreds of years after – Maharshi Patanjali formally documented sutras of Yoga in his book – "Yoga Sutras" and is referred to as the father of Yoga. Many gurus had worked time immemorial to propagating Yoga to the whole of the world.

Yoga is considered as one of the most valuable gifts of ancient Indian tradition to the whole world. Yoga is a spiritual discipline based on a subtle science which focuses on bringing back the attention from body consciousness to soul consciousness. Yoga has its root from Sanskrit word – "Yug" which means "Union" "to join" or "to unite". Yoga is a way of bringing in the harmony in your body, mind and soul. Regular practice of Yoga helps in experiencing the oneness of existence between an individual body and this whole cosmic world at large and the person who experiences this oneness is called "Yogi". It is believed that main aim of doing Yoga is to elevate individuals from the path of suffering and help them bring to the direction of freedom in all walks of life with experiencing peace, harmony and happiness.

FUNDAMENTALS OF YOGA

Yoga works on the body, mind, thoughts, emotions and energy level. Based on this, there are four major classifications of Yoga:

a) Karma Yoga is a way of achieving oneness between individual consciousness to supreme consciousness through the actions done by the body. You consider the body as an instrument for attaining the oneness. In the Epic Mahabharata, Lord Krishna had imparted knowledge of Karma Yoga in his lectures of "Bhagwat Geeta" to his follower – Arjuna when he had surrendered before Lord Krishna and refused to fight the battle of good vs evil with his cousin brothers – "Duryodhana" and family.

   There are various examples of Karma Yogis in recent time – Mahatma Gandhi, Mother Teresa, Dr APJ Kalam, Martin Kuther King Jr and Nelson Mandela's life have all attained oneness with the supreme soul through their actions.

b) Jnana Yoga involves using the mind as an instrument for achieving oneness with supreme consciousness. It is most difficult of four main paths of Yoga requiring greater inner will strength. The goal is to be free from the illusionary world of Maya to achieve the union of inner self/soul with the oneness of all life creator or supreme soul. It is the perfect path for sage, hermit or scholar.

c) Bhakti Yoga – involves using human emotions of love as an instrument to achieve oneness with supreme consciousness. It helps you to provide inner strength by taking you to the path of spirituality. It embarks you on your journey by visualizing the divine in all Gods' creations. It helps you to be at peace by accepting them in the way they are. We can consider Meera bai, Radha and various saints such as Tulsi Das Ji, Kabir das Ji, Guru Nanak Dev Ji as the perfect examples of Bhakti Yogi since they believed in peace and love for wider human community and nations at large.

d) Kriya Yoga involves balancing the energies in our body. It helps you provide the right direction to the life force, which is "the breath". With taking control of our breathing, we can control our state of mind, our emotions. Kriya Yoga is the systemic breathing technique which helps in harmonizing the body, mind, thoughts and energy.

In addition to these 4 Yoga types, there are other prevalent yoga types like Hatha Yoga, Dhyana Yoga, Rajyoga, Kundalini Yoga. Every individual can practice any or all of these based on his/her inclination and what they seek to achieve in life. Guru-Shishya parampara has been followed for centuries for getting insightful knowledge on Yoga in traditional schools. It is always recommended to have a Guru to start this spiritual journey since Guru guides you in the right direction by taking you ahead on the path of spirituality and self-exploration. Guru always helps you seek your goals or enables you to understand the purpose of the existence of life.

Based on my experience of practising Kriya Yoga from more than ten years, I can undoubtedly confirm that Yoga helps us improve specific powers within you.

Yoga helps us to improve our powers which we have

1) Power of Decision making: As we start practising Yoga, meditation and spiritual practices. Over a period, we observe that the overall strength of decision making improves multi-fold. There is clarity in thought process; your mind can choose the signal from the noise. It becomes easier to find what is the goal of life. Life looks like a clear lake with all the dirt settling at the bottom, resulting in seeing crystal clear water at the top.

2) Power of concentration/focus As part of my research, I got to understand a book: "FLOW" written by Mihaly Csikszentmihalyi. While reading his book, I understood, the human brain cannot process more than 110 bits/sec person. To hear anyone, your mind needs to process 60 bits/sec, that is the reason our brain can interpret and understand only one person at a time due to this. During my research while reading a book on Swami Vivekananda Ji, I got to realize that Swamiji had an incredible power of concentration and focus, he could read the complete book of more than 100 pages within few minutes. In one of the incidents, while Swamiji had one thick book in his hand and he was casually flipping through the pages of the book, and he completed all the pages in a few minutes. The individual who was near him asked: "Have you finished reading this book". To this, Swamiji replied, yes – I have completed reading this book. The fellow was surprised to hear that. To his satisfaction, he asked Swamiji a few questions from the book, which could not have been possible for replying without a thorough reading of the book. Swamiji was able to respond to all the questions correctly to that fellow. That is the power of concentration/focus which can be cultivated through the practice of Yoga and meditation on a regular basis

3) Power of unselfishness: Mystics or Yogis who have been practising meditation and Yoga for years together can echo this thought, Yoga helps you to sow the seeds of unselfishness in individual. A Person starts putting others life before thinking and caring about self. He becomes inclusive in his approach towards the world.

   Again, quoting Swami Vivekananda's life as an example. In this case, he was one of the unselfish yogis who had put his country before him. He always wanted to see India as a prosperous nation as it was earlier. He went to the US to propagate India's deep learnings of Vedanta to the whole world. Another example is Mahatma Gandhi, who always kept his country at the forefront of his thoughts and continuously worked for achieving its freedom.

   I can again think of Mother Teresa as one of those saints who kept serving the poor and needy on the streets of Calcutta and serving people was the motto of her life.

4) Power of Happiness – Yogis understand the true meaning and purpose of life. They always remain happy in whatever situations around them. Not only staying contented or happy by themselves, but they also spread this to across to the environment or society. Yogis understand that Happiness is an ultimate state of mind which get reflected in every act of their life.

Understanding the Equation of Needs and Responsibilities in Life

I will explain the fundamental difference between the concept of need and responsibility and how they are correlated with each other. Needs are referred to as what you want to take away from life and Responsibilities are referred to as what you want to contribute back to life.

Human being usually has six fundamental needs to be achieved. Although the quantum of these needs may vary from person to person. This is also stated and explained in Maslow's Motivation model as well[3]

1) The need for Certainty – Every individual always wants to have lived in an orderly manner—a place for everything and everything in place. We always want to have certainty in whatever acts we perform in our professional and personal life—the assurance of job, health and happiness in our individual lives.
2) Need for Variety – Nature has always taken care of need of variety. Every individual created on this planet earth is different than others, and every individual always looks for variety in life and get attracted to the different personalities. We can't live a monotonous life; we always look for varied experiences in life
3) Need for Significance – Human beings have the fundamental need of feeling important. It is expressed through the concept called "EGO" prevalent in every one since birth. They always feel to be rewarded or acknowledged for the work done. There can be two types of EGO – Positive EGO – which helps you take an extra mile in achieving your goals and Negative EGO which is self-destructor for individual, team, company, society and country at large.
4) Need for Love – Everyone on this planet has the inherent characteristic and need for getting loved by others. Love is the essential binding force for the existence of life. Parents love their children and family; children love their friends, belongings, so on and so forth.
5) Need for connection – Whenever two unknown individuals meet, they try to find the common link between them, commonality in behaviours, habits,

3 Maslow's Motivation model

thinking for better coordination. We, as humans always believe in networking and setting up connections. We feel more secure as a society of connected beings.

6) Need for growth – Humans always find the need for growth by learning something new regularly. They always focus on development and plan to move on to a high state of life.

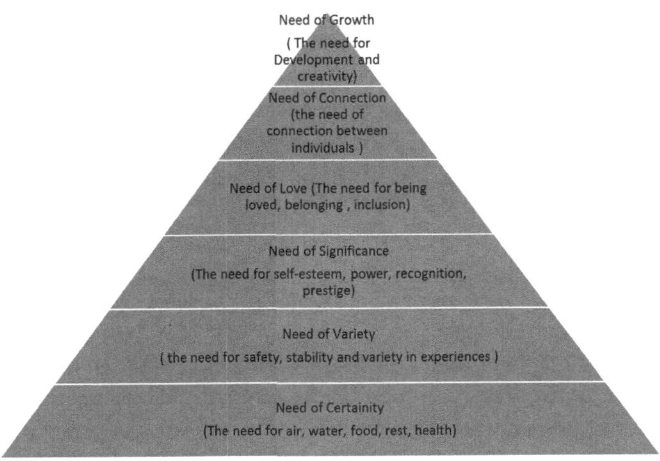

Responsibility is more of our actions which are bringing in positive impact/contribution in someone life or society at large. We need to understand the equation of Needs and Responsibilities as the Balance sheet of life. Taking responsibility makes us feel stronger and empowered. For Example – Why Our Prime Minister & President are one of those strongest people since they are responsible for the whole of India – 1.3 billion people – for their growth and well-being

Needs > Responsibilities (= Negative Balance in life)

So, with more needs, we are taking more from society. With fewer responsibilities, we are returning less to society resulting in a negative balance in life which causes more stress, anxiety, and fear. We will also find our mind restless in this case.

Needs = Responsibilities (= Zero Balance in life)

If we have our life needs equals to the responsibilities which we are willing to take in life, then we are just consuming the same amount which we are returning to society resulting into a zero balance society meaning that we will always be in a struggle to maintain this thin line of balance

Needs < Responsibilities (= Positive Balance in life)

If our needs are less, it means that we are taking less from society and with more responsibilities, we are returning more to the community resulting in a positive balance in life. With a positive balance of life, it brings happiness and peace in mind and sense of fulfilment.

Story of Businessman – focus shifts when we move out of the trouble.

While attending one of the knowledge and meditation sessions with Art of living –I got to hear this story. Here comes my version and interpretation of it:

Long long ago, there was a very Stringy businessman. He went to Kasi for getting rid of all his life sins by getting a dip in the holy water of Ganges. He had accumulated loads and loads of money and was one of the wealthiest figures of his time. He took the boat, and in some time, he was in the middle of Ganga. Suddenly, there was a massive flow of water, boat getting out of control, he got scared and thought that his life was coming to an end. He started praying to the lord that I had come to this holy place to get rid of all my sins and I had come here in your shelter, and now hey lord you were about to take my life: please help me….!!! Please help me…...!!!

"I don't want to die", with these thoughts in his mind and eyes closed, he started praying harder and harder. He was very much frightened by the sheer thought of losing his life. Pictures and memories of all his near and dear ones ran across his mind, as he thought his last moment was near. In his heart, he made a vow and told the lord that I would give all my wealth, savings and everything to you if you save my life this time.

Prayers on his mouth and belief in his heart, he was continuously chanting lord's name. Lord heard his prayers, thought of helping and blessing him out. Lord came in front of him in a disguised form – as a boat sailing helper and sat on his boat and started rowing his boat out of this turbulent water. Suddenly the businessman realized that he was getting out of the rough water and boat was coming back under control. The businessman opened his one eye and to his surprise, saw a man sitting in his boat who was trying to row back the boat to the shores. Businessman asked the helper: who were you and how come you got here in this boat; I had not seen you earlier. To this, the boat helper (disguised God) told that I was taking a dip in this holy water and when you were crying for help from GOD, and I heard your cry and thought of coming and helping you out. Suddenly the businessman asked: what else you heard from my conversation with GOD. Boat helper told me that I heard you offering GOD all your wealth and life savings if he protects your life during this turbulent time. The businessman was shocked, and now his mind stopped worrying about his life which was in danger a few minutes back, but mind started worrying about the promise he had offered to GOD for giving all his wealth and life savings.

The businessman told to boat helper that this was the offering I was making it to GOD, and since GOD himself didn't come, he sent you to help me. However, I cannot give you my whole wealth or life savings, but I would give you the half of it as I have to provide the rest of my wealth to my wife. Boat helper didn't reply anything to him but just smiled back. After some time, when the boat started moving closer to the shore away from the middle of Ganges, he told the boat helper again, "dear friend, I hope you would understand my situation, I would not be able to give you half of my wealth since I have a wife and four kids to take care of as well. Hence, I would only be able to provide you with only one-fourth of my wealth. Hearing this comment, boat helper still didn't reply anything and again smiled back at the businessman and started rowing back the boat. Again the businessman started thinking about this incident in-depth. He understood that what this boat helper was currently doing was just his job, as anyhow this man was swimming in the Ganges when I cried for help from GOD. He just overheard me and obviously when I was asking for help, it was his duty to come and help me, so he didn't do anything extraordinary in that. He just did his duty of helping other people, so why should I waste and share my ¼ of wealth and property with him, let me further negotiate it down. The businessman was also seeing that he was approaching closer and closer to the shore, so now his life was entirely out of danger. He again looked at boat helper, and he told him that since you helped me so much during my tough time, I would certainly reward you. Still, I could not give you ¼ of my wealth, as I have a wife and children and had some loans to repay, hence I would only be able to give you Rs 1000 which would be sufficient for you to carry out your rest of life peacefully. Boat helper still didn't say anything and again smiled back. Once the businessman reached the shore of Ganges, he put his hands into his pocket and brought back Rs 5 note and gave it back to the boat helper and told that since you helped me, I am very thankful you and anyhow you live near the Ganga shores, money would not be of much importance to you. You, please have this Rs 5 note and live your life with happiness. Businessman handed over Rs 5 note and got out of the boat, and boat helper took the money and laughed and gave back the Rs 5 note to the businessman.

After hearing this story, I had multiple takeaways: when human is in deep need from GOD, he equates his life to the most precious earnings/valuable things of his life, but as he gets more relaxed, he starts equating the value of his life to such a minuscule level which is not even worth anything. Life indeed is such a priceless phenomenon and gift; it cannot be equated to anything else. We need to have Guru in our life to help us stay afloat in his ocean of life. What a better phenomenon – if your mind becomes your own Guru and a guiding force for the whole of your life.

With this thought, let's dwell deeper into this concept of GURU now.

MOST POWERFUL 3G'S (GURU, GRATITUDE AND GRACE)

In this world of 4G or 5G technology, let me bring your focus on the most basic 3Gs of life. These 3Gs helps you operate your life effectively and efficiently.

Guru –

First G (Guru) is the most potent and deep-rooted in each of us. Guru is made up of 2 words in Sanskrit. Gu + Ru. "GU" means darkness, "Ru" means a person who removes darkness around you. In all our ancient scriptures such as the Upanishads, Guru has been described as a person who helps to remove darkness from your life, helps you to provide liberation, helps you to show the correct path and acts as a leader for you. There is a very famous Sanskrit shloka: "Gurur Brahma, Gurur Vishnu, Gurur Devo Maheshwareh, Gurur shakshat param Brahma, Tashmay Shree Guruvey Namah". During the Dvapara Yuga – Lord Krishna acted as the GURU for Arjuna and guided him by imparting him with the knowledge of karma- Yoga during the battle of Kurukshetra between Kauravas and Pandavas. Lord Krishna gave knowledge of Bhagwat Geeta to Arjuna in the most challenging times. Words of Lord Krishna in the form of Bhagwat Geeta are relevant as of today as well.

In Indian culture, we celebrate a Guru's presence by a special occasion – "GURU Poornima", which is always a special day for all the knowledge seekers of life. As per the ancient Vedic Hindu astrology, Guru (Planet Jupiter) is referred to as the biggest and most powerful planet in our Solar system. Guru (Planet Jupiter) is more than 11 times in diameter than our planet Earth (Prithvi), and its volume is more than 1300 times that of our planet earth, which means that it will take more than 1300 Earths (Prithvi) together to make Guru (Jupiter Planet). Due to its immense size, Guru (Jupiter planet) has such a high gravitational pull that it protects our planet Earth (Prithvi) from various meteors and meteorites approaching it. It is believed that if the planet Jupiter (Guru) didn't exist, our planet Earth would have been destroyed by so many meteors or extraterritorial bodies hitting us.

Guru (Planet Jupiter) acts as a protection shield for our planet Earth (Prithvi). Same is the role of Guru (teacher) in the life of an individual. Guru shows the direction to all the individuals in the path of spirituality and well-being. Guru glows like a candle to remove the darkness of ignorance in an individual's life and brings enlightenment.

We are fortunate to have been protected by the many Gurus throughout our lives – starting from Planet Jupiter (Guru). When a child is born, he or she is protected by the parents in his/her childhood. Hence Parents acts as the first Guru for the child by providing proper nourishment and care for his/her well-being. As we grow, we gather knowledge from teachers (Gurus) by going to school or college.

So, Guru is not referred to an individual or person; it is more of the force which helps you to move ahead in life whenever you are feeling stuck at any point in time. It is more of a life force within each of us which helps us to learn anything new in life so that we can grow as a more mature and satisfied human being.

I want to share a story of Dr APJ Abdul[4]; he died delivering his last lecture in IIM Shillong. During one of the conversations between Dr Kalam's adviser – Srijan Pal Singh Ji and Kalam sir, Srijan Pal Singh Ji kept asking Dr Kalam; please tell me what you would like to be remembered for? President, scientist, writer, Missile Man, India 2020, Target 3 billion or what?

Dr Kalam replied: "as a teacher", and finally he was in the end moments of his life, and he was in an education institution delivering his last lecture of life.

That's the power of the GURU or teacher in life, Guru or teacher transforms the lives of so many individuals during their lives.

Gratitude

2nd G refers to as the Gratitude; it is very much needed to lead a peaceful life. Gratitude refers to the feeling of gratefulness for the availability of all the desired resources around us. We must feel tremendously lucky that out of so many planets in our solar system, it is only planet Earth which has the atmosphere or environment suitable for living a healthy life. When we have the expression of gratitude towards whatever we receive in life, we always feel contented and satisfied from the inner being. The feeling of Gratitude always brings in more of expansion in you, and you feel connected with the sense of oneness.

Grace

3rd G refers to as Grace is the most powerful as it makes drastic changes to your life, with grace you can start feeling the abundance in life and ensure that all happiness and sense of fulfilment flows in your life. Grace referred to as "Kripa" in Hindi, makes your life full of ecstasy once you start observing it.

---

4 https://www.businessinsider.in/neither-president-nor-scientist-apj-abdul-kalam-wanted-to-be-remembered-as-a-teacher/articleshow/48251886.cms

MEANING OF A-U-M SOUND

AUM is the most primordial sound in nature, and it comprises of 3 significant sounds –

1) Sound of AA
2) Sound of UU
3) Sound of MM

When any seeker is looking for basic meditation can use these sounds individually to achieve the benefits of the same.

When you start chanting AA sound, it helps you activate your lower chakras, primarily the sound of AA travels in the downward direction in your body toward your naval, stomach or abdomen and even down. According to ancient Hindu beliefs – Brahma is considered as the God for the creation and in our body "Brahma Tattva" lays in the lower body parts like the stomach and below since they create lots of energy by burning the food. Even the reproduction system, which is responsible for the creation or giving birth to new life, is situated on the lower body part. It is believed that if we chant AA sound for 7 or 11 times on regular basis, it enhances your "Brahma tattva" in the body, meaning that person would be good in more creative jobs (E.g. Architect or interior designers).

When you start practising UU sound, it helps you activate your middle part of the body where your lungs or heart is present. Sound of UU is referred to as "Vishnu tattva" since it is associated with maintaining and preserving the life forces. If you observe closely, all our life-preserving organs like Lungs or heart are situated in the middle part of the body. Regular chanting of UU sound helps you to enhance your Vishnu tattva. It is believed that a person with high Vishnu tattva would be good in the job roles like being a doctor, support engineer, carrying out maintenance and support staff.

When you practice MMM sound, it helps to activate the Shiva-tattva in the human body. When a person closes his/her eyes and chants the "MMM" sound, the sound mostly stays in the upper body part, predominantly in the head region or above the neck to head position. This activates the Shiva-tattva. The people who have higher Shiva tattva are good at handling transformations or good troubleshooters.

When we combine AA-UU-MM sound, it results in AUM sound, which helps you balance out all the three life tattvas – the creator, the preserver and the transformer. Practising AUM sound regularly brings peace and harmony in your body, mind and soul. Hence the AUM sound is considered very primordial and helps you improve the "Prana" levels in the body.

AUM story

During my research, I went through a lot of literature and documents, and as part of one of advance meditation session with Art of living, I came across a short story worth sharing. Here is my interpretation and version of sharing this.

Once there was a Guru and Shishya during ancient times. The shishya was very loyal to the guru and was regularly following all the instructions given by Guru. Shishya approached Guru one day and told that he wanted a secret mantra. The Guru asked him to work for some more time and follow his instructions, and he would share that secret mantra with you. Shishya went away happily and worked for Guru for some more time. Guru called back Shishya and told that I am now happy with your devotion and I would share the secret Mantra with you. Guru said that please bring your ears closer to my mouth. I would share it directly in your ears so that no one else could hear that and Guru uttered the sound of "AUM" in the ears of Shishya. Shishya thought it to be a secret mantra felt quite happy after receiving it. Shishya went to the jungle and sat under the shade of a tree and started chanting AUM mantra, and to his surprise, he heard back the sound. He thought there was some echo; he moved to some other place as well. He again chanted AUM and heard back the sound of AUM coming to him. He got confused about that. He opened his eyes to see from where the sound of AUM was coming. He saw that there were so many people who were chanting the "AUM" Mantra. Shishya felt cheated; he thought of going back to Guruji to tell him that Guruji didn't share any secret mantra with him. AUM mantra was all known with others as well; hence it was no secret. Guru told Shishya that he had only shared this with him, but he also said that in this world there are many gurus like him and there are many Shishyas like him as well. So, Guru said that some other guru would have shared this secret mantra to their shishya and hence this mantra would no longer have been hidden. Shishya was still not looking convinced with the reply of his Guru. Guru Ji anticipated this. He went inside his hut and gave a small piece of material to his Shishya and told him that it's a precious material. Please go and try to find the value of this precious material. Guruji told him if he could go back to the village and try to find the value of this precious material correctly, I would give you a new secret mantra. Shishya being happy again went to the village nearby to find the correct value of the precious material. He first went to the vegetable seller and showed him the precious material, Shishya asked the vegetable seller what value you could give it to me for this precious material. The vegetable seller told that the weight of this material was close to 2KG hence he could exchange it with any food item worth 2 KG. Shishya got confused with this reply. He remembered that Guruji told that it was a very precious metal, and this vegetable seller was only giving me 2KG food item in exchange for this metal. With the confused state of mind, he went ahead and met the potter who prepared mud utensils. Shishya showed this metal to the potter and asked him the value of this metal. He told that this metal could be of some use to him in making some lovely pottery. Potter told he could give back few mud utensils in exchange of this. Shishya still got confused, and he remembered what his guru mentioned that it was a precious piece. He now went to the blacksmith to check the value of this metal, blacksmith saw it and told that it could be made into few sharp weapons, so he told that he could give him few weapons in exchange of this metal. Shishya said that these weapons would not be of any use to me and he took back the metal from him. He went back to the cloth-seller, asking the value of it. Cloth-seller told it was of absolutely no use to him. In the end, after the full day of roaming in the village, Shishya was very much frustrated and was remembering what his guru told him, and he tried his last luck with a goldsmith. He handed over the precious metal to the goldsmith. Goldsmith immediately recognized the value of this, and he asked the shishya – were you any king or any thief, Shishya was shocked to hear these words, he never anticipated this kind of reply from Goldsmith. Goldsmith told that it was so precious material which only a king or thief could afford to have. King would need this material to have it as an antique collection in this courtyard or thief could have it if he would have stolen it from the king's palace.

After hearing these words from Goldsmith, he understood the value of this material, he went back to his Guru and asked him to forgive him. He told that he understood the importance of this sacred mantra "AUM".

AUM, as a sound is an invaluable resource. The practitioner of spirituality can only understand the real meaning or importance of this. This could be used as the best tool for easy meditation by anyone. By chanting it for few minutes, it brings clarity of thoughts in mind and body.

JOURNEY OF THE INNER WORLD (STAY HAPPY, STAY BLESSED)

We are always good at dividing the world into two parts – Have's or Have-not's, Rich or Poor, developed or under-developed, calm or restless. Most of the time the division is based on the material or wealth or possession which any individual, state or country holds and these notions of material wealth keeps on changing with every day passing by the stock-market ups and down, economical turbulences, external world shocks. Still, there is a whole world which always lays unchanged within you. There is something very fundamental in every individual, which forever remains the same throughout the life journey from the day when you were born till the time of your last breath.

Let me give you a new perspective to introduce you to the whole new world, which is quite different. There is the **Outer world** – which keeps on changing on a regular basis, which you have a very little control on – your office, your work, your colleagues, your place, city, state, situations around you; and the **Inner world** which holds the secret sauce for success and happiness in your life if you handle it well.

There are so many fundamental theories of change management which keep on saying that change is the only constant, and we need to change our self and adapt ourselves to survive in this highly competitive world. With so much of the work and time being always spent on managing the outer world effectively, we always try to manage and respond to the external world through our five primary senses, body, mind, memory, intellect and ego. Our very self which is our inner world always remains unattended for years and years altogether. We don't hear our inner soul due to this noisy outer world. Practising Silence or "MAUN" is another powerful tool for going deeper into your inner world by detaching yourself from the outer world

Yoga is the fundamental way of connecting your body, mind and soul. It helps you to bring in the harmony between your inner and outer world. It teaches us the fundamental point of how to live in a state of happiness.

Most people associate Yoga with the physical body and Asanas for keeping it healthy. They forget the point that Yoga works both at the gross and subtle level of existence; it is just that we need to have an awareness of this beautiful inner world. Once you have taken up the journey of the inner world which is so peaceful, calm and serene. You will not find anything so beautiful in the outer world.

Another fundamental part of life is our breath which we always take it for granted; this is the first and last thing we do as we come to this world or leave this world. It is the bridge between the gross body and subtle existence. We daily consume more than 10,000 litres of air which is an immense amount of intake of anything we have in a day, and we are still so insensitive towards it since our breathing happens effortlessly, 24*7 without us paying any attention to it. Our Breathing is the most significant source of energy in our body in addition to the food, water and sunlight which nourishes us.

So, the science of breathing is the connecting dot between the outer world and the inner world. It helps in converging both the worlds together. It is through this most powerful tool in the world that we can change our state of mind from being unhappy to happy, anxiety to being calm. This is the thread which holds the key for bringing in inner transformation, and if we are happy and peaceful from inside, then the outside world unrest does not bother us, and we enjoy every moment of life. If we are not satisfied with the inner side, then what so ever great opulence lays outside, we will not be able to enjoy it.

So, the journey of moving from outer world to the inner world aimed at creating harmony in everything we experience is the art of creating an awareness towards our breath which helps us stay happy and blessed forever.

PART 3

ANSWERING TOUGH QUESTIONS

> Do not over-indulge in eating, sleeping, working, social activity or in any activity, no matter how pleasurable it is, for an over-indulgence will yield nothing but unhappiness.
>
> – Paramahansa Yogananda

I AS LIFE CENTER

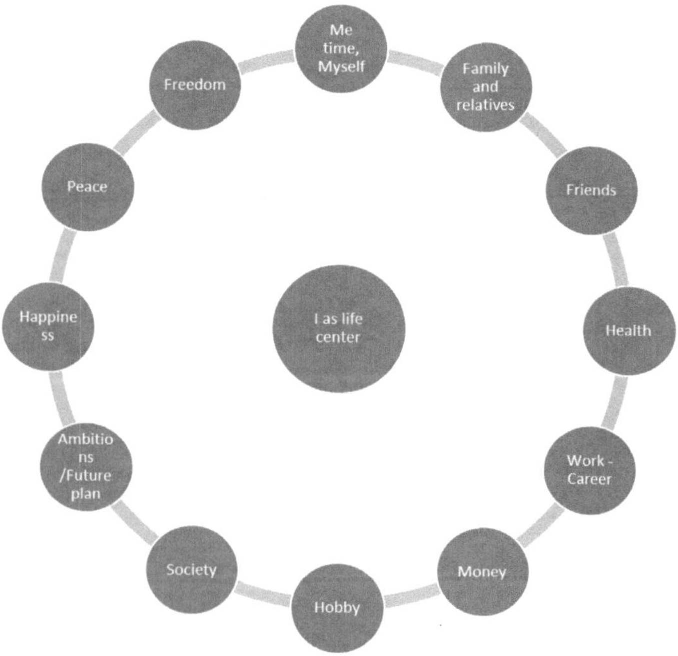

I got introduced to this concept of Life Centre during one of the leadership summits wherein I heard Sneh Desai (Motivational speaker) talking about this. In this chapter, the idea of "I as a life centre" is being discussed. If we observe our life very closely, we can correlate it to all 12 aspects, wherein we all have a sense of belongingness since these elements are all related to "I as life centre". These 12 elements are like 12 milestones or diamonds of "I- Watch", wherein "I" is still in the middle and is getting impacted by some or all these elements as they are surrounding this "I".

- **Me or Myself time**: We all have been living our lives based on the influence of our parents, society, relatives, family, friends and others. But if we segregate all these other elements: can we define what is "Me or Myself time"? Probably most of us would not have even thought about it. As we see our lives as a child, when we are born, we are the most creative of all during this phase of life. We still don't know how to talk, but we communicate the most actively with our parents and family. They can understand our needs and demands, although we formally don't know any of the languages except the language of love. We are the most expressive during our initial phase of 0-12 months. We are the kings of our own will. We rule the world in our own terms. We decide the sleep patterns of our family. We determine our own time for eating and getting freshened up. Whole life revolves around us as we are the centre of attraction, and we are the happiest of all creature on the earth. Have you ever seen a small child – he is most contented, satisfied, full of life and happiness. But subsequently, when we start going up, we are guided by our parents or elders for the way of living, way of eating, way of studying, way of behaving. With so much of information being fed from all directions, the raw creativity of child or the self-exploratory nature gets halted all of a sudden, and the child always starts feeling that he/she is suddenly bonded by life principles – early to bed, early to rise makes you healthy wealthy and wise. Healthy eating habits and so on and so forth. We start leading the mechanical life as we get programmed by our surroundings, including family, friends, relatives, society at large.

- In this all mad rush of life – "BEING" part of "Human BEING" get lost somewhere, and we just remain as "HUMAN". Bringing back the focus on SELF or ME, exploring the real purpose of life in this journey is crucial. Most of us – "our lives" get consumed as a raw material in this industry/factory of "life", which we later realize or understand that we have become polished products from Life factory and have lost all our earlier characteristics of RAW MATERIAL. There is no harm in getting consumed and transformed from RAW MATERIAL to be FINISHED PRODUCT, but this FINISHED PRODUCT should not start considering his/her life as "FINISHED". When we get processed from the factory of life as "FINISHED PRODUCT, we get so much tightly programmed that we lose all our creative thinking and flexibility. The dilemma of life is we get to realize this when we encounter some unprogrammed challenges in life. That is the reason why most of the people fail and lead a mediocre life since none of us is taught to have an inner focus on self. With so much discipline or life programming, we all become outward-focused rather than the inward focus. Although we certainly can't control people, situations and activities around us – but if we are taught to have internal focus- we can have better control on ourselves to handle these situations, by not reacting to them, but rather reflecting for a moment and then responding to it.

So, whenever life gives you a googly, we all have an inbuilt pause button which we should all be aware of and use it to handle our life in a better manner. Every problem has a solution, provided we have the will to solve it.

Storytime – Lock, Key and Hammer

Once upon a time, Hammer was having a discussion with Key and was saying to him, you are so small and feeble as compared to me, I am much stronger, bigger and tougher than you. But whenever It comes up for the opening of the lock, I keep on hitting and making several hard impacts on the surface of the lock from outside, but it does not open. But you are so small, yet whenever you touch lock, it always gets opened. To this Key replied to hammer, you always try to break or transform the lock from outside, and I always focus on changing the heart of lock – deep within, hence locks open-up when I go inside, and it resists whenever you try to impact it harder from outside. Similarly, all our lives are like a lock, key and hammers

Solution for any problems of lives can only be searched deep within, and transformation of life can only happen by self/inner reflection.

- **Family and Relatives**: With changing the demographic structure around the world, the concept of family and relatives have changed drastically. Thirty years before, more families used to be joint or extended families. Due to increased cost of living, now in most of the cities, we usually see the concept of Nuclear family – Husband, wife, one child. With just three people in a home, it has been now called family. With the pace of city life, husband, wife don't even get a chance to talk to each other daily in case both are working. They are not able to devote time to their child. All wait for weekends – Saturday and Sundays, thinking some magic will happen for spending time with all, but honestly, nothing improves. Time just keeps on flying. We see so much stress and differences and fights these days. Families getting split apart.

In current times with so much stress and turbulence around, it certainly makes us think of the old family structure – joint or extended family. Humans are still a social animal, they still need people around them to share their talks, anger, frustration, and it is the concept of the joint family which comes for rescue in these challenging times. Joint families share the workload of taking care of little ones in the family by elderly ones. There are better bondages with people of different age groups – grandparents, parents and children around. Also, it helps you create better value systems in the younger generation. Virtues of tolerance, accommodating other ideas, respecting other thoughts get inculcated in them.

When children grow up, there are so many stories or memories for them to share if they are brought up in joint families.

- **Friends:** Friends are also one of the essential pillars of "I as a life centre". If we closely observe our lives, most of us have our best friends during the time of childhood and best memories while spending times with friends. I am sure: all of us still cherish the days of our school – Those are the most beautiful times of life with friends all around us. When I see my daughter currently in school enjoying her school day, it always brings me back to my school days memories most vividly in my mind. With time as we grow-up, schoolbooks, get converted to competitive exams books, friends get converted to competitors. We all start getting crushed in this mad race of getting admissions for higher studies. You get admissions to professional degree courses; you become more like worrying about your future, job and professional life and circle goes on. Nowadays, friends are more about the count of the connection on FB or other social media platform. All of us have thousands of connections on these social platforms, but can we all call them friends or just connections. Do those connections matter to us? Whenever we see pictures, comments, like on social media platforms, we start comparing our lives with them and slowly with the feeling of comparison in our heart, feeling of loneliness also creeps in. We all connected on this superficial world, but when we look deep into our heart, still the connection with SELF is missing. We always try to connect outwards with the world, and we never pay attention to have connection/ friendship established with our mind or heart. Our mind can certainly be our best friend in this time of loneliness to give us the guiding light for life.

Make your Mind you best friend

- **Health:** Health is the most important and yet most neglected aspect of "I as life centre". "Health is so cheap that it is available for free, but we still don't value it, diseases are so expensive that people buy them". Most of the current health issues which humans are facing all around are majorly due to life-style disorders. Too much usage of mobile phone in daily life is also causing various health hazards. In recent time you would have heard about below issues due to excess uses of mobile phones:
    - Cell phone Elbow, Cell Phone Wrist
    - Text Claw, Text Neck
    - Impaired Memory
    - Hearing Sensations losses
    - Restless thumb syndrome
    - Carpel Tunnel Syndrome
    - Lower Back pain [5]
- Stress being the major contributor and silent killer of all. If we see around, nature has provided us with the most beautiful gift for healing ourselves in the form of sleep. We need to practice the concept of "Healthy Body and Healthy Mind" by having proper sleep and meditation practices.

5 https://balakishore.in/digital-wellness/

For healthy living, we need to have a daily routine to ensure our body follows a cycle.

As we grow-up, there are multiple chances of developing different lifestyle-related diseases such as diabetes, Cholesterol and others.

We need to strictly regulate our food and diet habits to ensure us to live a long and healthy life.

The example of health consciousness can be learnt from Japanese, where average life expectancy is 80+ years which is more than the world average life expectancy. Health is also related to earlier discussed factors: Me time, family, friends and relatives. Individuals who are more social and have a great network of friends, family, relatives will have a longer life span.

- **Work -career**: With the advent of the 1st Industrial revolution in the late 18th century, there has been a concept of mechanization which had been prevalent in the world. Humans started moving from Agrarian society to more industrial society. There had been a mass migration of people from villages to city. Countries around the world started planning their cities to bring all comforts and amenities to residents of the cities. Suddenly there was an uneven distribution of the human population around the different parts with the creation of different industrial hubs. With inventions of newer and sophisticated means of production/ assembly line, the concept of "BLUE-COLLAR" and "WHITE COLLAR" workers emerged. Concept of 40 to 45 hours working duration per week gained momentum with the advent of the 3rd Industrial revolution. Outsourcing gained the momentum with work getting done beyond the boundaries of countries of origin. There was a rise of the knowledge economy. Power of internet and Personal Computer ruled the world for later 1990s onwards. The social fabric of families got evolved into more nuclear families. Concept of joint families became a distant past.

Starting of the 2000s onwards, there is furthermore focus on SMAC: the concept of Social networking platforms, mobility, analytics and cloud got prominent. From the flat and connected world, the world turned into VUCA – volatile, Uncertain, complex and ambiguous. With slightest changes in the globe resulting in a widespread impact on global economies had the potential to create turbulence around the world. The world had seen multiple recessions, the transformation of social and economic fabrics.

We are now in an era of Industry 4.0, in coming days, we can anticipate complete change in the ways of living, with AI, ML, IOTs competing with humans in the space of jobs and with so much data being created around the world, new kinds of work concept will emerge. Concept of traditional jobs will no longer be there, and the focus would be now on getting the work done rather than human. Different Social fabrics of trust and collaboration will also evolve.

With so much unpredictability around you, there is one thing for sure – new dimensions of exploring life and redefining new paradigm will evolve. Future certainly holds great promises for a new generation of millennials who are now more empowered with the power of digital technologies and transformation all around them. More and more people are now turning out to be entrepreneurs – Job creator rather job seekers in the coming world. Concept of "I as life centre" needs to be better prepared for handling these changing dynamics around the world. The best way for handling the tougher time is going back to your basics or roots of origins – turning the focus of self to inwards and practising concepts of "SAVERS" – "Silence, Affirmation, Visualization, exercise, reading and scribing" to have better control on life and self.

- **Money**: Money is just an instrument to exchange and realize the value of transactions between two different parties. Before the advent of money, for thousands of centuries, people used to use the barter system to exchange their product for fulfilling their needs. The person who had an excess of food grains used to exchange it with Potter to get pots and utensil and similarly blacksmith would exchange his produce against the items of his needs, the world survived and evolved from those days. With different civilizations coming into actions and discoveries of different metals in earth crusts, more formal way of trade and exchange used to happen through precious metal coins. Trade markets and trade routes got established around the world. During the times of Great Kings – coins of different metals such as copper, gold, silver become prevalent in the world. Different world economies started growing. Subsequently in later 1700's or early 1800 -formal paper currencies got introduced. Central authorities such as banks were established to protect the interests of nation-states. Trade got more regulated, with the concept of mass production/mechanization – different countries looked out of their geographic boundaries, and the concept of colonization became prevalent. The United Kingdom became one of the most powerful nations in the late 1800s or early 1900s. Different wars were fought in the world to gain access to territories. The world had faced two world wars and multiple civil wars resulting in causalities of hundreds of thousands of people. Establishment of organizations such league of nations and subsequently "United Nations" resulted in ensuring greater peace on the latter half of the 20th century. Adam smith – father of the modern economy - had written in his book: Wealth Of

Nations – quotations from the book: "Wherever there is a great property, there is great inequality".

The world had seen the rise and fall of nations from an economic perspective. Still, if we closely observe the nations on the scale of spirituality – there is a lot to achieve for all countries for managing its human race in a better form.

We have always been taught to be money-earning machines, rather than satisfied or contented human beings.

Humans are always focused on accumulating more and more of fiat currency, rather than spiritual currency in the form of love, contentment, peace and happiness. The success of any nation-state is measured by its GDP growth but not by the mental health of people living in those countries. It is time to change the world from being more materialistic driven to be more spiritual driven world because, at the end of life, we all need to face the GOD in the form of the Balance sheet of life – Karma's or acts which we have done to uplift our soul. We need to be more soul-conscious rather than body-conscious. Hence "I as life centre" need to invest time on earning more and more spiritual currency rather than fiat currencies of the world.

- **Hobby:** "I as Life centre" develops different kinds of hobbies to fruitfully spent the idle time. The time which is left after spending it on your work, family, friend and yourself. Different individuals have different kinds of hobbies. Some of them expose their creative side by hobbies such as drawing, painting, dancing. At times, these hobbies, when practised regularly, can be transformed into your career goals. What could have been a better choice if we love the profession which we do. Every individual is different from others in terms of their capabilities, learning abilities, creativity. It can be the greatest gift to self if we can create the hobby of meditating. Whenever we get any idle time: we can certainly practice it with eyes open or closed and by bringing attention to the breath.

- **Society:** "I as life centre" has not only a role to play for the overall wellbeing of an individual but also society at large. Society is a very closely knitted fabric by different kind of people living at that place. At any stage of a nation's history, the progress of humankind can be truly reflected by the type of society around. Individuals work hard to earn name and fame for themselves in the community. He/she wants to be known to others by means of actions which he is doing for the overall well-being of society. If we closely observe all the successful people after attaining name and fame, they always want to contribute back to society. Whether it is Tatas or Birlas or Azeem Premji: all big corporate houses, they run philanthropic trusts to reach out to broader people for contributing back. We have examples of philanthropists like Warren Buffet, Bill and Melinda Gates foundations which are working around the world on different social issues and upliftment of people in under-developed and developing countries by being part of various vaccinations and health safety drives. Various NGOs or Non-profit organizations such as Art of Living, Isha Foundation, Brahma Kumaris and many more are working across the length and breadth of multiple countries to create awareness on the overall well-being of society at large. These organizations are working on creating awareness among people of various critical social issues such as addressing climate change issues by reforestation and planting trees, saving rivers by reviving them, propagating organic farming practices, education for low-income families. "I as life centre" also have a responsibility to play in this big picture for the overall wellbeing of human society. As the more we take responsibility, we feel more empowered to bring the change in society.

- **Ambitions/ Future**: "I as life centre" always think about the future, but the fact is Present is inevitable, and it is the moment to be lived in. We all plan to make our future bright and prosperous. In this race of securing the future, we don't care for our present. We stop enjoying the present moment. We have to start living our present in the best possible way, as present holds the key for the future. If "I as life centre" is happy, contented and peaceful in the present, no matter what lays in future, it will not worry me, since I understand the importance of living the present moment.

We can't change the circumstance around us, neither our friends, family, or social life. We can control none of them. The only thing which we can at least take control of is this body and mind "I as life centre". If we make a promise to ourselves and be well prepared to handle anything which comes to us, then indeed all the worries of future get melted away. We certainly need to make this as our ambition of life that: "I as life centre" make a promise to myself to have full control of my body, minds, thoughts and actions. I would observe every action, thoughts of the mind and "I as life centre" is in complete control of my actions. If each of us starts taking full responsibility of at least "I as life centre" and make it an ambition that future is never a cause of worry for me, the world would be more of transformed place with no stress around.

Also, we need to pass on the same message to upcoming generation as well: we see children as old as 5 or 6 years are feeling depressed, lonely, started worrying about future, which is not a good signal. Dream of transforming, the stress-free world is only possible when the upcoming generation starts understanding the value of life. We need to cultivate the seed of hope, possibility and optimism: Next Generation should believe that "Future has unlimited potential to explore and definitely will be better than today and yesterday".

- **Happiness**: Let's try to evaluate happiness from the lenses of spirituality. Happiness is not the occasional aspect. It is the very nature of us. When we start living in body consciousness state, we get impacted by things, situations and circumstances around us. But when we understand ourselves as "SOUL consciousness" we indeed find this as an innate quality of us.

Let us do a basic experiment and test for us: If we closely observe our life: "I as life centre" lives our life in instalments. We make promises to ourselves that I will be happy when I will have a house or when I will have a car or when I will have a promotion or when I will get married or when I will be blessed with a baby. We always try to correlate happiness with these milestones or occasions and when we achieve these milestones or experience: we become happy for the momentary time and then start chasing the next milestone. We don't consider this life as a journey where each moment is different and will never repeat; each moment needs to be lived to the fullest in happiness. Hence life as a phenomenon can't be a momentary or occasional aspect; instead, it is the very nature of "I as Life centre" we need to realize this. The moment we have the realization of this, we become liberated from all shackles of life which we have created around us.

The moment we understand that we are "SOUL consciousness", we get transformed into eternal nature, and we feel ourselves as Powerful.

When we live in body consciousness, we look at the quality and experiences of life-based on our limited physicality of the body. With physical body is all you correlate to. Desires are inevitable, and this constant longing for desires is like a vicious circle, makes us starts chasing our shadow, whenever there is an unfulfilled desire, it will create misery because we get so caught in that desire that we begin considering that desire as a whole world. We forget the distinction between what the true nature is of "I as life centre".

Gautam Buddha in his first lecture after enlightenment also talked about 4 Noble truths

- The existence of suffering
- The cause of Suffering
- The cessation of suffering
- The Eightfold path

Gautam referred to as desires and cravings for it as the cause of suffering and then subsequently in lecture unfolds the path for getting rid of this suffering.

It is always referred by different learned scholars, masters and realized beings – it is ok to have the desire since we being a human being in "Body consciousness" will associate our self to cravings, but this obsessive and compulsive nature of the mind to start considering these desires as Life centres and starts living around it creates problems. When we understand the distinction that desires are just a minuscule part of existence, and if we can roll-in and rollout these desires as per our will, then we become masters of ourselves.

Now Let's evaluate happiness from the perspective of modern psychology. I tried researching this topic of happiness from psychology aspects as well. I happen to listen to the TED talk of Mihaly Csikszentmihalyi[6] wherein he was discussing FLOW as the secret to happiness. He explained few of the concepts of how people feel when they are in FLOW: he described how some of the music composers while composing music get so engrossed in the flow to reach the new reality – the moment of ecstasy that the person/music composer starts feeling as though he does not exist. I can completely correlate this experience of the non-existence of the body to be in the state of SOUL consciousness, where you always feel blissful and ecstasy. There are multiple other examples stated by Mihaly Csikszentmihalyi for people reaching the state of FLOW: poetry composer – S Perry, Anita Roddick, Masaru Ibuka – which can also be

---

6 https://www.ted.com/talks/mihaly_csikszentmihalyi_flow_the_secret_to_happiness#t-1462

correlated to the moving away from body consciousness state to soul consciousness state.

In his discussion, Mihaly states when you are in a state of flow, you feel and believe:

- Completely involved in what you are doing, you feel completely focused and concentrated
- Individual get filled with a sense of ecstasy – of being outside everyday reality
- Individual experience greater inner clarity – knowing what needs to be done and how well are we doing
- The individual feels that activity assigned to him is doable and we have the adequate skills to perform the task
- A sense of serenity arises – there is no place for worries about oneself and individual feel of growing beyond the boundaries of the ego. Ego melts or disappears.
- In the state of FLOW, individual feel timelessness. The individual feels like time is flying – hours seem to pass by as minutes
- An individual has intrinsic motivation to carry out the task

So, if we observe, when an individual is in state of flow: he pumps in everything of him to it – energy, thoughts, mind – complete attention is on that task. Hence the outcome of this state is bound to be happiness.

Based on my understanding, I see complete congruence between views of modern psychology (Concept of FLOW) and spirituality of achieving happiness in life – which is such a fundamental need but so challenging to achieve for many.

- **Peace**: Peace is again the very nature of "I as life centre" – Soul. To experience and experiment it – if we closely observe anyone sleeping, you always find him very peaceful. That is the true reflection of self. Let us watch a very small child, maybe a couple of months old, he doesn't understand the world around him, you can always observe the peace, content, happiness around him. The very reason is although being a child of say 1 or 2 months, he is still not completely aware of "BODY consciousness". Most of his actions are the result of his true nature. All of us are blessed and born with this innate nature of being peaceful. In this dust of life, there are multiple layers that get covered around us, and we often miss out experiencing our essential nature of life.

Many a time, we want to go out in untouched nature or out of our home to experience the peace, some of us experience it when they are doing any tasks which they love to do. Realized beings have feelings of blissfulness and peaceful while serving and helping others.

When we start exploring our true nature as "SOUL consciousness" – we always find peace in each aspect of life. You need not run around or go to different places to experience it. Peace is like a shadow which is always there with you. You just need to be mindful of this.

Also, whenever "I as life centre" express or experience anger, we feel something in us, which is contracting, whenever we are peaceful or happy, there is always a feeling of expansion. Our consciousness expands more and more when we are experiencing peace.

- **Freedom**: Freedom can be referred to as liberation or Mukti in literal terms; it means getting a release from any boundaries of life. Let's experiment whenever we identify or associate ourselves with the physical body or boundaries; we will always be longing for freedom from these limited boundaries to unlimited or boundarylessness. Hence, sense of physicality creates the edge and distinction, with that the continuous desire of breaking away from the limitations of physicality arises. This is more of phenomena about "BODY consciousness". When we have this realization that we are not limited with any boundaries of the body, we are powerful, peaceful, loving, blissful Soul with no limitation of bodies, we can experience the immediate freedom within.

Freedom is all about realizing your true nature and being always associated with your true nature. Then indeed, there will not be any desire for freedom.

Sincere seekers of life can also refer to freedom as understanding the real purpose of life as well. All of us being sincere seekers in this journey of life needs to understand the fact that we are just like actors in this stage of the world, coming out and performing our role and exiting when our part is over. The only thing within our control is giving 100% in the part which we are playing. When we have the realization of this feeling, we don't have any longingness or unfulfilled desires in us.

3C'S – SECRET OF HAPPY LIVING

I happened to attend one of the knowledge sessions of Guru Guar Gopal Das in Pune. I was completely impressed by the learnings shared by him. He talked and shared about life philosophies in straightforward three easy to correlate rules:

Secrets of a happy Life – 3 C's

- **Power to Choose**: Situation or Problems happen automatically, happiness is certainly a choice
    - Life is full of options and abundance. All of us are blessed with this natural gift of taking a pause and choose the best-suited response.
    - At the time, we knowing or unknowing allow others to remote control our emotions, we certainly need to overcome this tendency in life.
    - If you are facing a problem in life and have a solution to overcome it, then why worry? Apply the answer and get rid of the problem.
    - If you are facing a problem in life and don't have a solution to overcome it, then why worry? Since you don't have anything in your control. The best thing you

can do is – have faith and trust on "Supreme Soul/ Parmatma". He will take care of you as a child.

- **Power to Change**: we should change our attitude towards life to be more contented. Don't hold on the past.
    - Your attitude will define your altitude or journey of life. It is always required to have a positive attitude. This is easier and obvious to have a positive attitude in the favourable situations of life; the depth of great character is always known when we maintain a positive attitude in adverse circumstances of life.
    - There were two fishes in 2 different water glass tumblers looking at each other – Bigger fish was in a smaller water tumbler and a smaller fisher in a bigger water tumbler. When bigger fish was looking at the smaller fish, it was feeling unsatisfied as it was seeing a smaller fish enjoying in a bigger tumbler, where smaller fish had more space to move around. It hardly had any room for moving in the smaller tumbler, whereas when small fish looked at the big fish, it was also unhappy as it thought how small I am, as compared to this big fish. So, contentment or discontent has nothing to do with your current state of life. It is more your state of mind or overall attitude towards life.
    - Most of the times: Fights happens in life because we consider I am correct, and you are wrong. We try to change others opinion by forcing our views on them. It is ok to have different people having different thoughts. We should start respecting their viewpoints, be inclusive and at peace with them.
    - Whenever someone shares a joke with us, we laugh at it once we hear it for the first time. If the same person keeps repeating the joke, again and again, we lose the interest in it, and we don't laugh at it next time. Still, for any pains or sorrows of life, we keep playing back the records/cassette of painful memories again and

again and don't feel bored listening to them again from our memory. We should flush out these negative and painful thoughts and memories from our mind. Change is the only constant in life.

- **Power to Control**: we should control the tendency to compare in our life
    - We always have this tendency to compare every aspect of life. Most of the time, this tendency results in unhappiness, stress, unsatisfaction and other negative thoughts in life. We certainly need to control this tendency; otherwise, we will always find that the "Grass is greener on the other side of the pasture."
    - If we want to compare, let's compare yourself with people who still don't have basic things in life to live that will instil in you the attitude of gratitude towards the life and will make you more contented and happier
    - If you look upon someone as inspiration and work hard to achieve something like him, then this comparison acts a motivational force for you to live your life better.

ANSWERING THE MOST POWERFUL QUESTION – WHO AM I?

> The Spirit running your life is sacred, honor this LIFE ENERGY. As you honor it, all other virtues will become your expression effortless
>
> – GURUDEV SRI SRI

I got to understand about the depth of this easy, yet the most challenging question of my life – Who am I? During one of the "The Art of Living – Happiness Program" – I got introduced to this most trivial yet most important question. Understanding this question has helped me change my perspective towards life and made me more of a sincere seeker for the whole of my life.

An individual is usually identified and associated by the name their family has provided them, the work or position they are holding, the role they are playing and so on. Society associates them with the religion which they are practising, the region where they are staying, the nationality they are holding or the qualifications which they achieved over a period. None of these attributes truly define the original identity of an individual. These are more of the nomenclatures through which individuals associate themselves.

If we go deeper in the sense of self-exploration – Who am I – question: we can still find commonality among all the individuals: all of us observe different kinds of emotions (love, anger, hatred, ecstasy etc.) which may be Positive, Negative or Neutral emotions and thoughts during 24hours' time. Hence, we all are connected beings observing multitudes of feelings and thoughts.

If we go more in-depth at the existing levels of human beings: we have the following seven different layers of existence from physical to subtler level.

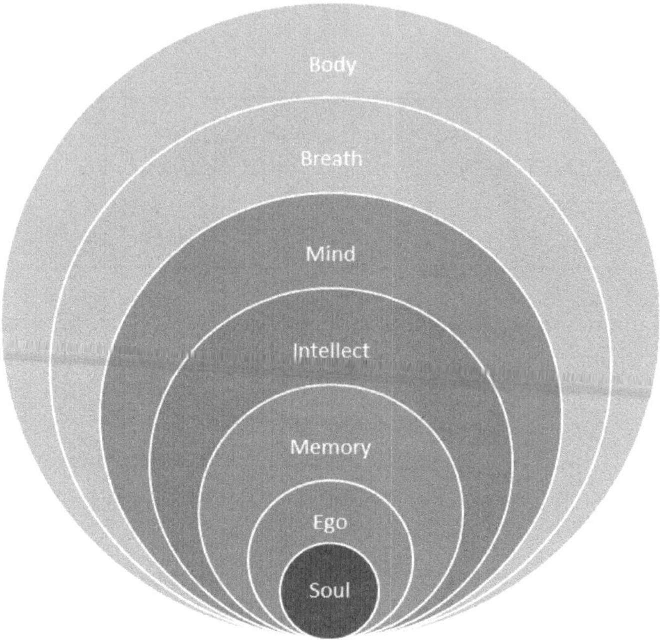

- **Body**: This is the most obvious element of existence as we can visibly see it. Hence, it can be called as existence at Gross level
- **Breath**: We had started breathing when we made our entry on this world, and it would be the last activity which we will do while leaving back our gross body on this earth. Breath is like a constant flow, which runs automatically without being even paid attention to it. The elementary and fundamental level for doing meditation is paying attention to and regulating your breathing to make your body feel relaxed. If we deeply observe, breath has a connection with our mind. If we can regulate our breath, we can control the thoughts in our mind – we can improve the overall quality of thoughts and remove the unwanted ones.

- **Mind**: Mind is not equal to the brain. The mind is the powerhouse for the creation of all the thoughts in this world. It is like a production house creating all different scenes of the movie of life. The mind is also the creator of this world. Since everything is first made in this mind and then it gets manifested in actuals.
- **Intellect:** Intellect is again a more subtle concept; it helps in decision making for human beings.
- **Memory/Impressions**: Constant, repeated impactful actions create memory or impression. Not all actions create memories. Some very trivial Actions do not get stored as memory, as they are automatically flushed out. Imagine if we would be able to remember and store every action starting from birth, then the whole memory system would not be able to manage the sheer size of it all. Nature, being an intelligent phenomenon, selectively creates memories out of impactful actions.
- **Ego**: Ego is again a more profound phenomenon related to "I", our ego helps us perform different roles in life. When we play the role of father, brother, son, or husband, we have different egos or masks to carry out those tasks effectively.
- **Soul (Self or Atman or consciousness)**: Soul is the primary identity for all of us. As we peel off each layer of our existence from body, mind, intellect, memory, and ego, we understand our true nature – ever peaceful, loveable, blissful, happy, pure and potent.

In simple terms: if we compare the Human body as a computer: we can classify it into three categories: Hardware, Software and Electric Current.

The body can be considered as Hardware. Breath is equivalent to power/ electric current which runs this machine. And the Mind, Intellect and components below (memory, Ego, Soul) can be equated to software which certainly needs constant upgrades for better functioning.

For good maintenance of the body, we should practice Asanas,

For regulating our breathing, we should practice Pranayama

For sharpening of Mind, we should practice Meditation

For experiencing the soul consciousness rather than body consciousness, we need to practice meditation regularly.

Let's try to understand the relationship between Body and Soul. The Soul is after all the ultimate owner of this body

If we see a pearl and its shell, the more value is of a pearl rather than the shell which is just the covering and holding it. Similarly, let's take an example of a Car and the Driver. In this case, if the driver is driving the car, the soul can be considered as the driver and body can be correlated to the Car. So like the driver driving the car, it is the soul who is driving this body and the ultimate owner of this body

> You are a living, Perceiving, knowing BEING who is in a body. As an infinite being, there are two things that will determine your fate – Choice and awareness
>
> – Christie Marie Sheldon

Explaining the Concept of Soul: Story of "Raja- Janaka": "Who Am I."

Long Long ago, during the time of Treta Yuga – there was a very learned, wise and powerful king – "Raja Janaka". He was considered as the most spiritual and intellectual seeker of that time. This story is about his journey of self-realization. One day, Raja Janaka was in his court during the long day – managing his kingdom's daily work and affairs. He was so tired that he thought of taking a quick nap. As he dozed off, in his dreams, he saw another ruler attacking his kingdom. Raja Janaka lost the battle and had to surrender after that. The other king asked him to leave his palace and his kingdom immediately. He was completely shattered due to this shameful defeat and started roaming around a lot. At one point, after walking for many days at a stretch, he grew very hungry and thirsty. He reached at the gates of a house begging for a Roti when to his surprise, he found that the village was suffering from drought. With people having nothing to eat and hardly anything to drink, he looked towards the sky and asked GOD for some mercy.

A passerby took pity on Raja Janaka's condition and offered him a piece of his Roti. When Raja Janaka was about to bite into that Roti, an eagle flying above swooped down and snatched away the portion of Roti from Raja Janaka's hand and flew away back in the sky. Completely shattered by this act and thinking of his imminent death, he cried out loud with eyes full of tears. And with that, Raja Janaka woke up from his dream amidst the proceedings of his court. All the court members suddenly looked at him and were shocked by his expressions and loud crying. He felt awkward and murmured to himself: "Is this the truth, or was that the truth?"

Raja Janaka adjourned the proceedings of the court for that day and went back to his palace. He still had the same thoughts running around in his mind. He didn't attend any other court proceedings for the next few days and was continuously thinking and murmuring the same words: "Is this the truth or was that the truth."

This court incident spread like wildfire, and everyone came to know about this incident. One of his very respectful ministers was very concerned about the state of mind of Raja Janaka. So after gathering some strength, he went to Janaka's palace and tried asking him the question while the Raja still kept repeating the same words. He then sent many Gurus and learned scholars to Raja Janaka's palace to consult with the Raja and help them solve this mystery of his murmurings. Ashamed of his dream, Raja Janaka was not ready to share anything with anyone, and none of the Gurus or scholars was able to understand and help him out in that situation. Suddenly the minister came to know about sage – Ashtavakra passing by Raja Janaka's kingdom. Sage Ashtavakra was one of the most accomplished sage/mystics of his time who had immense knowledge of the Vedas and the Brahman. On a special request from Raja Janaka, Sage Ashtavakra agreed to meet him. Sage was a profound scholar, and he knew the situation of Raja Janaka. Janaka said the same words with Sage: "Is this the truth or was that the truth". He didn't want to share this dream with Sage. Sage immediately replied: "This is not the truth nor was that the truth. He who is observing this here and was observing that there is the only truth". Raja Janaka immediately came out of that dilemma. There is detailed conservation which happened between Raja Janaka and Sage Ashtavakra: this dialogue is referred to as "Ashtavakra Geeta."

"Ashtavakra Geeta" is considered as one of the best conversations between a seeker of truth in the form of Raja Janaka and Ocean of knowledge – Sage Ashtavakra". It is said that during this conversation itself all the doubt of Raja Janaka got clarified, and he attained enlightenment by having the clarity and understanding of the "The Most powerful question – Who am I."

> *When you see events as just happenings, rather than as doings, you are liberated right away*
>
> *Ashtavakra Gita*

Three Faculties of Soul

During one of the advance knowledge session with Brahma kumaris team – Sister Chitra, Mukesh sir and others, I got to understand this concept deeper. The soul is not any physical identity; it is more of metaphysical concept, which is the ultimate owner of the body, Soul imparts its functions through its faculties:

Three faculties of Soul:

- Mind
- Intellect
- Impressions

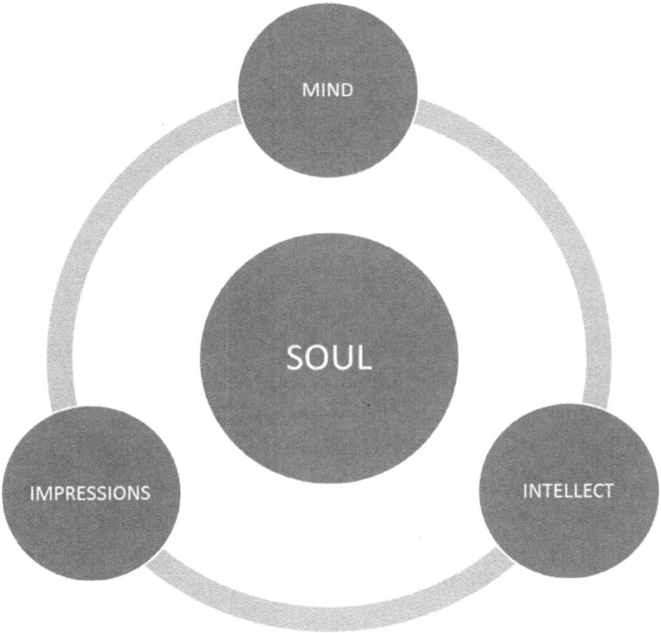

Mind – Creator of Thoughts

The mind by itself is neither good nor bad. Turn it outwards to desire the objects of the senses and it binds. Turns the same mind's passions inward to seek the lord, and it frees a man forever : BHAGAVATA PURANA

People often confuse the mind with the brain. They both are not the same. The mind is again a metaphysical concept, so the primary function of the mind is to generate thoughts. If we observe our daily life, we get thousands of thoughts; thoughts keep on continuously popping up in our mind any or every time without us even controlling it. So, the most important thing is to know how to handle the quality of thoughts? Or the question can be: Can we maintain the quantity and quality of thoughts? The short answer is YES. Regular meditation helps in controlling the same.

Also, Mind works based on the concept of Image or visualization. Hence there is a well-known concept called mind mapping. Whatever you feed into the mind by visualization, it creates mental circuits based on those imagines or visualizations, and these visualizations become strong when you practice them regularly. Meditation works on this concept of mind visualization because whatever you want to be, or achieve, you perceive and visualize it regularly as part of your daily meditations. You see yourself slowly transforming into those and subsequently over a period of time: the individual becomes what he or she has been visualizing regularly. This can also be explained by an example of the placebo effect.

Nocebo effect Vs Placebo effect

Your mind will adjust the body's biology and behaviour to fit with your beliefs. If you have been told that you will die in six months and your mind believes it, you most likely will die in six months. That is called the Nocebo effect, the result of the negative thoughts which is exactly opposite of the Placebo effect, wherein healing is mediated by a positive thought.

What you think you become, what you feel you attract. What you imagine you create.

Everything that is created in this world by humans, it was first created by your thoughts, beliefs and ideologies and every judgement you have ever made in your mind. Hence Mind is called a beautiful servant and a dangerous master.

Never allow your mind to control you on these five things:

- **Your past**: since you can't change anything of the past, there is no point in living in the past or keep remembering about it. The best thing is: learn from it and apply the learnings in the present or future if required.
- **Other People's opinions**: Never be a football of other people's views as you can't control other people's thoughts, or beliefs, hence their thoughts/opinions should not impact you much as your life is your life, it is none of their life.
- **Limited Beliefs**: No one in this world is perfect and knows everything. Everyone is human and living their journey of life through their limited belief systems. Hence you should never be carried away with someone's limited belief system. You are the best judge of your life; therefore all your actions should be decided by you and not to be influenced by others.
- **Relationships**: relationships are the best gift of god to all of us; hence we should stop judging people around us, whether it is the relationship between a parent or child, husband or wife, brother or sister, friend and other friends, the essential thing which is part and parcel of relationship is the trust for long term sustenance
- **Money/Wealth**: Money or wealth will never be enough for anyone on this earth, how much ever you accumulate it, your mind will always want more and more, so there seems to be no end to it, so never get trapped in the traps of mind for name, fame, money and wealth since it is a never-ending vicious circle.

Four Different Types Of Minds

During one of the advance knowledge session with Brahma Kumaris teacher – EV Girish sir, I got to know about four different types of mind

- **Conscious mind**: Conscious mind is what we are aware of things which are happening around us during our daily activities, tasks are done during the waking hours. We experience the outer world in the wakefulness state through our conscious mind. Whatever actions we do through our body, say eating, sleeping, reading, watching TV, playing, are all activities done through the conscious mind. It is around 10% of our mind

- **Sub-conscious mind**: Sub-conscious mind lies below the level of conscious awareness. Its physical seat in the body is - the lower brain and spine. It is called a Little deeper mind. Whatever we repeat regularly, gets recorded in the sub-conscious mind. Let's assume you are driving a car and talking to someone on the phone and you know your home is near-by on the left turn. You are still talking to the person on the phone, but sub-consciously you give left indicator and turning your Steering wheel on the left, although you are still deeply engaged in conversation on the phone. You are still on the phone, and you came out of the car, locking the car perfectly and start walking towards your building. You arrive at the lift lobby area and press 8th floor, where your flat is, while doing this you are still talking to the person on the phone. All these activities which you were doing without paying any attention is done due to the stored procedures in your mind, due to repeated activities. It is the main reason of how we think and act.

  Let's take one more example: let's assume someone is speaking in a public event and the next turn of speaking is yours. Once the first person finishes his speech, and the moderator announces your name, you suddenly start feeling jittery and shaky hands. You know from inside that you are feeling shaky, although no-one can see/ notice it from outside. You are still trying to laugh and pretend as if you are normal and Ok. This feeling of shakiness is arising from some of the thoughts of fear or unpleasant experience of public speaking in the past stored in your subconscious mind. It is like the Autopilot mode of the mind, which get triggered without your awareness. Our habits, our pleasant and unpleasant experiences get stored in the subconscious mind. Our sub-conscious mind is certainly more potent than the conscious mind.

Here are real-life examples of it:

- Michael Phelps: greatest swimmer ever in the history of swimming. He used to practice himself with a thought – how would he swim if his goggles leaked during swimming and it happened: In 2008 Beijing Olympics, in 200-meter butterfly swimming, his goggles leaked, so he relied on the feel of his imagery to know where he was and when and how to stretch for the finishing line. He had trained his sub-conscious mind so well that he finished strong and won another gold medal, setting a world record
- Olympic Gold Medal winner Lanny Bassham also trained his sub-conscious mind to win the world championship in Seoul. His words were: "Though I could not go to the shooting range, I did continue the training, I simulated shooting for 2 to 4 hours in a spare bedroom, a technique called dry firing, I won the world championship that year in Seoul.

Sub-conscious mind contributes to 50 to 60% of the mind; it helps us in achieving what you want. It is an essential part of the mind, and the most important thing is how our thoughts can be controlled through the sub-conscious mind. Sub-conscious mind can be rewired to bring positive thoughts through meditation.

- Unconscious mind: We can understand the concept of the unconscious mind by this example: let's assume, we went to the surgeon, and we want to get some part operated due to some ailment. The surgeon cannot do the operation in the same state; he/she first applies anaesthesia, so that we stop feeling any physical sensation in that part and then operate on it. So unconscious mind can be considered as that state wherein there is no interplay between your sensory organs, outside and your consciousness. In an unconscious state, your conscious mind is not working at all.
- Supra Conscious mind: supra-conscious mind can be referred to as being the SOUL consciousness state having the original sanskara of SOUL (7 innate qualities). 30-40 % mind: When we stay in the supra-conscious state, then we are free from body-consciousness, it is like experiencing infinity within you.

There is saying by Dr Emoto Massaro: Critical thinking without hope is cynicism. Hope without critical thinking is naïve. This world is filled with wonders and mysteries that get more incomprehensible if we try to think of a reason. Except for some of the fundamental things, no one disagrees that there are still so many unknowns.

As part of his experiment on water droplets for almost 20 years: he has showcased that water when exposed to loving, benevolent, and compassionate human intention results in aesthetically pleasing physical molecular formations while same water when exposed to fearful and discordant human intentions results in disconnected, disfigured, and "unpleasant" physical molecular formations

With this experiment, it was evident there is so much of power of thoughts and emotions on water, imagine how much it can transform or affect human bodies if used positively.

Maharishi Effect[7]

The power of thoughts is allegedly so mighty that they not only affect us, but when harnessed collectively, can change the outcome of the society as a whole. This phenomenon is termed as Maharishi effect. In one of the studies, it was reported that when 1% of the community that practised meditation, the crime rate was reduced by 16% on an average

For a healthy mind, it is crucial to have:

- Less quantity of thoughts
- More quality of thoughts

As thoughts are equal to the energy flowing in our minds, if the energy flowing is in a random manner or directions, then the overall result will not be very substantial. Hence, we should regulate both the quality and quantity of thoughts, and the good news is that we all have the power to control them.

There are multiple sources of thoughts which get generated in our minds:

Sources of Thoughts

- Sensory inputs – Whatever we experience through our five sense organs- Eyes, Ears, Nose, Tongue and Skin acts as an input and stimulus for generating thoughts in our minds
- Belief Systems: Belief system is again a significant contributor of thoughts in our mind, it is commonly said: whatever you believe, you become that.
- Past Memories: Memories also contribute to some extent in terms of creating your thoughts in mind.
- Creativity: Creativity also leads to different kinds of thoughts in mind, so if you are architect or writer or

7 https://research.miu.edu/maharishi-effect/

professional photographer, your quality and quantity of thoughts will be completely different than another person who is working in say software or IT industry or who is working in manufacturing organizations.

During my enlightening interactions with Sister Shivani (BK)[8] in one of the knowledges sharing sessions. I got to understand that we should never under-estimate the power of thoughts; it is the most incredible path to discovery. We can tune our life the way we want if we ultimately realize and understand the power of thoughts. There are majorly four different types of thoughts:

- **Positive thoughts**: Positive thoughts are those who provide us with the experience of our original nature of self or soul and are universal in nature such as feelings of peace, love, purity and power. Positive thoughts make us internally strong to handle any situation in life. You can always feel the flow of positive energy or aura of people who have positive thoughts as an integral part of their life. Practising it regularly, it has the power to bring transformative changes to human life and their surroundings.
- **Necessary thoughts**: Necessary thoughts are referred to thoughts which are needed for your survival or completing your daily tasks. These thoughts may differ from person to person as it is more related to your lifestyle – personal and professional lives of individuals. These thoughts are needed to address your fundamental needs such as those related to work, food, family etc.
- **Negative thoughts**: Negative thoughts are the ones which impact not only you but also your surroundings negatively; hence these thoughts should be avoided entirely from the mind. These thoughts harm health

8 https://www.speakingtree.in/blog/4-types-of-thoughts-that-impacts-everyone

– both physical and mental. Negative thoughts are based on the five vices – lust, anger, greed, ego and attachments.

5 Vices causing Impediments of Life

During one of the knowledge discourse sessions with experts from Brahma Kumaris, I got to know about these five impediments of Life, which I can completely correlate to. This is a natural phenomenon for all. The most important part is how to overcome these impediments and come out of it unaffected. It can only and only be possible through the power of "Self-realization". Once it was asked to Buddha during his knowledge discourse with his disciples: what have you gained by renunciation and meditating for so long? He gave a straightforward and beautiful answer, "I gained nothing, but I have lost these five impediments of life."

- **Lust**: If we check the basic definition of Lust, it is defined as uncontrolled psychological force producing an intense desire for an object. Lust can be for sex, money or power. It is basically an unchecked force of nature, which at times results into sinful actions or long-lasting sorrows and pain.
- **Anger**: Anger is again expressed as a negative feeling, in which you consider someone has done something wrong. It is more of a feeling that I am correct, and you are wrong, and things are not happening my way. In various chores of life, sometimes individuals get angry over very trivial things leading to bigger conflicts and issues resulting in greater loses in life. The biggest irony is most of the times individuals don't even consider being in a state of anger for a long time is problematic and resulting in severe health issues

    - **Greed:** Greed is also used in negative connotation: when an individual has an excessive selfish desire for wealth or power. Uncontrollable greed results in individuals doing wrong acts and later resulting in repentance.

    - **Attachment**: Attachment is more of neutral feeling: which results in more of binding with other-self. It is about holding back to situations, circumstances and people in life. Individuals are having deep attachment with relationships, pleasant emotions, memories and even materialistic thing resulting in greater craving and longing, which is the cause of suffering in life. We certainly need to have – "LET IT GO" attitude to avoid unnecessary suffering in life.

    - **Ego:** Ego is again more of neutral or negative feelings. Ego is usually associated with excessive possession of individual self-esteem. There is a very slight differentiation between self-esteem and Ego.

- **Waste thoughts**: Waste thoughts are the ones which end up resulting in wastage of your physical and mental energy which in turn result in you feeling drained out. Wasteful thoughts get generated by unnecessary gossips and too much worrying about the future. We can certainly plan for the future as it is unpredictable, but unnecessary worries can result in wasting energy.

As you start paying attention on a daily basis on the quality of your thoughts, you can certainly eliminate the negative and wasteful thoughts and focus more on Positive or necessary thoughts.

Here is the simple formula of managing thoughts:

(Promote)Positive thoughts >>Necessary Thoughts >> waste thoughts > Negative thoughts (eliminate)

Focus your efforts, time and energy more on culminating Positive thoughts during your 24 hours. Necessary thoughts usually come effortlessly as they are related to the basic instinct of life; hence you need not worry about generating essential thoughts. You should purposefully avoid wasteful thoughts and forcefully try to eliminate negative thoughts as they are the poison of life for you and your surroundings.

To culminate the habit of generating positive thoughts, you need to make your mind as your best friend and try to ensure every day whenever you wake up in the early morning, to have a focus on the following six habits. All successful people around the globe have practised these habits.

SAVERS

These six habits can be remembered through this acronym: **SAVERS.** This is not a new concept. Concept of SAVERS has been widely thought, discussed, researched by leaders around the world. I got to read about these from the book "The Miracle Morning – the not so obvious secret guaranteed to transform your life before 8 am – by HAL ELROD."

- **Silence**: Regularly practising silence in the early morning whenever you wake up. Make this a habit to spent time with yourself, spent around at least 5-10 mins in silence before you start gearing up for the chaos of the day. This is as good as sitting in a meditative posture and be with the mind for some-time, making it your best friend. This helps in improving positive thoughts during the day by eliminating wasteful and negative thoughts in your life. If you closely observe Indian culture, philosophy or spiritual journey, this concept has been regularly practised since 100s of years. Saints and Rishis used to wake up early in the morning and used to sit and practise meditation, to tame the mind and nourish it for flourishing it with Positive thoughts throughout the day. Nowadays, with technology all around, the first thing which we do is check our mobiles, and when we start checking our mobiles, automatically thoughts start pouring into our minds based on the subject which we see in the mobile. As soon as we wake up in the morning, we should purposefully avoid the habit of checking our mobiles and try to remain in the meditative or friendly state with your mind – the best friend of your life

- **Affirmations:** Make truthful affirmations and craft your affirmations as your commitment to getting them manifested. Daily Positive affirmations play a vital role in every individual's life. It helps in creating a mental image of your future. It is always said: things get created twice in life, once in imaginations, and then the second time, you see the manifestation of the same in actuals. Many successful actors in real life have done this art of affirmations which has brought dramatic changes in their lives.

- **Visualizations:** Use visualization to motivate yourself on a daily basis. Your Mind understands the language of Images and constant repetitions. Hence it is always important to have mental Imagery of **what** you want to become and how you want to see yourself. Create mental images of you being successful, full of love, happiness, and it starts getting manifested over a period of time.

- **Exercise:** Give your physical body a boost by doing exercise or Yoga Asanas. This is very important to be physically fit. If we want to spend our whole life healthy with our body 24*7*365, it is at least needed to spend some time 30-40 mins every day doing physical exercise or Yoga Asanas for taking care of your body. It helps in avoiding the ageing of your body. It is always great to do Upa-yoga for all body parts starting from the top of your head to your toes, as we are only able to work properly since all our body parts work in a synchronized manner.

- **Reading:** Read at least a few pages daily and make it a habit like all successful people. Be it CEOs, business leaders, or celebrities, they all take their time out to read books of great writers as a practice, in addition to generic routine reading. Reading gives you a depth about the subject and widens your horizon for understanding of matters of life. You start appreciating life and diverse perspectives and become more inclusive. Your character reflects the kinds of books you read; hence we need to be very specific and demanding while selecting the book title or author. It is always said: Being alone is better than being in bad company, and Books are the best company for anyone and everyone. Books help you to remove your loneliness and allows you to connect to your inner core.

- **Scribing**: Clarify your priorities by scribing daily: It is always recommended to scribe down your goals of life – long term, medium-term and short term and create daily priority lists based out of that. In many studies, it has been proven that visualizing is not only essential for achieving anything but Scribing, writing it down on the piece of pen and paper and creating a plan out of that goals can lead you to the destination. The only visualization can be equivalent to "DAYDREAMING", but actioning it in out objectively by creating the plan is the way of achieving it. As part of affirmations and visualization, you will have a firm commitment to your goals to succeed in life. It is scribing, which helps in answering the most challenging questions of life:

    - Why: Why do you want anything? Why do you want to achieve this goal?
    - What: What would you do to achieve it? Listing down the set of tasks required to do this.
    - When: When do you want to achieve it? Tangible outcomes with defined timelines

INTELLECT

Functions of Intellect: Decision maker

- Comprehends: Whenever we receive any information from the channels of our sensory organs, intellect tries to understand the information received by validating it with past information.
- Discerns: Discern is the power to recognize or find patterns based on the present and past information patterns
- Discriminates: Discriminate is the power to differentiate, distinguish between what is correct or what is wrong based on your current and past information stored
- Decides: Decide is the power to arrive at a conclusion by considering all the aspects in totality
- Analyses: Analyse is the power to examine methodically in order to explain and interpret it
- Chooses: Choose is the power to pick between different available alternatives in front of us.
- Calculates: Calculate the power to arrive at a conclusion based on the data made available to the intellect

IMPRESSIONS

Impressions are the deep routed impactful profound memories, habits, natural gifts stored in your mind

Attributes of Impressions

- Memories: If we observe our mind, it is one of the greatest filters. It does not store anything or everything. We have been doing our daily routines such as brushing our teeth, taking a daily bath, getting freshened up, eating food three times a day, but do we remember every one of these activities such as what I have eaten one month back? Ideally, the answer is "NO". We don't store each action in our memory. Memories are created by anything which is distinctly different from our normal ways of life: any delightful or horrible experience.

- Habits: Habits being good or bad are created by repeated actions which we keep on doing. Initially let's assume we start learning a car, we pay 100% attention to driving it correctly by putting the complete focus on Accelerator, Clutch, Brake and Steering Wheel. Over a period of time, if we start driving the car daily, it becomes part of our habits and over a period of time, driving a car becomes so effortless that we don't even remember when we have inserted the key and started driving. But certainly, we might still have memories of our 1st car driving experience. It is tough to change habits as they are created over a period with regular practices.

- Instincts: Some of the individuals are gifted with capabilities of having special instincts available since their birth or childhood; these are due to impressions of past births.

- Speciality: Few individuals have gifted with some specialities such as knowledge of Vedas or Sanskrit language knowledge from childhood, great dancing or singing capabilities. These traits are carried over as impressions from previous births

- Nature: Few of the Individuals have very distinctive nature since their childhood. Some are very aggressive, others are introvert and soft-spoken, yet some others are extrovert and blessed with great public speaking skills since childhood.

Sources of Impressions/Sanskars

Impressions are usually attained through the following sources:

- **Past birth:** As per religious and spiritual beliefs, a soul takes multiple births on this earth. Due to multiple births and law of karmas and past actions, some of the impressions get carried forward from the past birth to your new birth.
- **Parental:** Some of the impressions or sanskars a child receives from his or her parents, family and upbringing. Hence it is always said that we should focus on providing great Sanskars to children during their formative years of life
- **Company/ place where you live:** The place where you are born also creates an impact on the child.
- **Present:** Your current actions or karmas which you do knowingly or unknowingly create an impact on you and help you to form up your future. This is the most powerful source as actions result in building up a great character of life.
- **Eternal:** There are seven innate lasting characteristics of the soul, which is always there in every individual who is born on this earth.

The Neuroscience behind Sanskars formation

I had heard so many people saying that they have been meditating since so many years, but still, they are not able to see any transformational changes in themselves; their habits are still the same. How to answer this tough question? I too was wondering about this in my journey as a sincere seeker, and I got to understand the answer to this question during one of the knowledge sessions by Mr Bala Kishore Ji. They have been actively working on this subject for so many years.

What is a Sanskar/Impression?

As mentioned earlier, there are various ways to define them – Say deep-rooted habits, old habits, attitude etc. It is a learned behaviour repeated over a period. For example: getting angry, jealous or sulking. I am sure all of us want to change these negative Sanskars or impression. Good news is, these can be changed over a period. Let's go deeper into this aspect to answer this question.

Let's understand: How we learn any basic thing? What is learning?

Let's understand if you learn English words today, what happens tomorrow? You forget them. Only when you start repeating them again and again, you remember them. The first step is to acquire the information and the second step is to store the information in a safe place in memory and then constantly recalling them. If any of these steps are missing, then learning will not happen.

Neurobiology of Learning & Memory

Inside the brain, there are about a hundred billion neurons. These are the workhorses that help in remembering something.

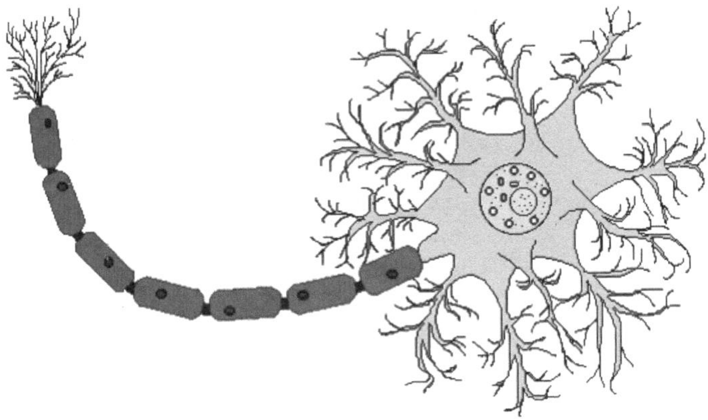

The above diagram is the primary functional unit of the brain. Three parts of the brain – cell body, axon (long-tail) and dendrite.[9]

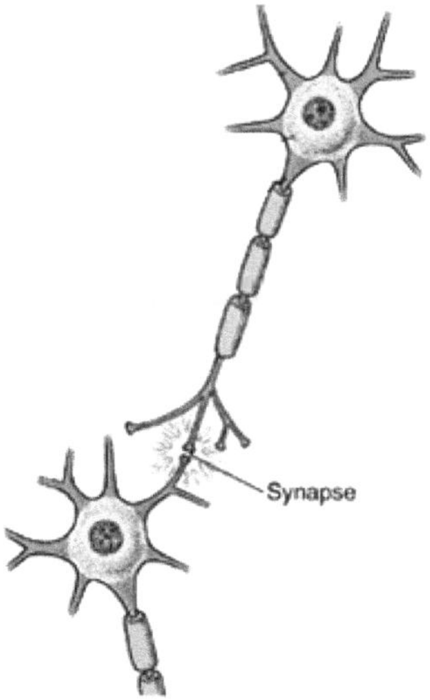

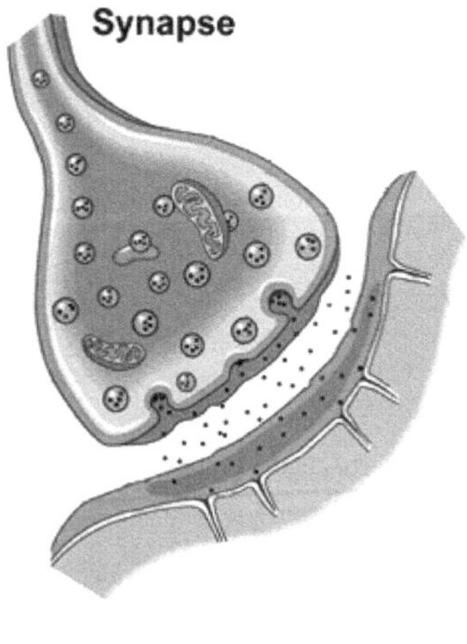

9 https://balakishore.in/articles/neuro-science-behind-sanskar-formation/

The brain comprises of 100 billion neurons. Each neuron can get connected to about 10 thousand other neurons. There is a small gap called synapse between any two neurons. When information starts getting exchanged, that is when chemicals start flowing between two neurons, and we say that there is a connection established. And only when a connection is established it means you have learned something. That is, a bit of information is stored in memory. So, you have learned something only when the corresponding neural networks are formed inside the brain. Whenever you learn something new, a new set of connections are formed inside the brain[10].

Have an Interest in any Area/ Subject

To form a new set of connections, it is very important to have an interest in that area. If any person reads a book without having an interest, there will not be any new connections established in your brain since it will not be registered in your brain.

If any person goes to a cinema hall, he/she watches the movie with will attention or concentration because the movie content interests the person. Same is when you are watching your favourite TV series, it is your love for the content, which helps to create complete attention/focus or concentration to that subject of interest. So, your love and interest to any area or subject help the brain absorb and retain the information easily, resulting into the creation of these neural networks and these neural networks get strengthened with constant usage of these subject areas. When you continuously recall any subject, these neural circuits strengthen more and more. In case you don't constantly use/ recall these neural networks, these neural networks become weak. Now we understand the logic of saying "Practice makes a man perfect" – by making these networks stronger and making the recalls easier.

10 https://balakishore.in/articles/neuro-science-behind-sanskar-formation/

Three insights for Sanskar transformation

- Interest in a subject is needed to create a new neural connection
- New information leads to new neural circuits
- The more we use the neural circuits, the stronger they become, and it becomes easier to recall.

Let us consider our brain a simple green patch of land with grass. When we start learning any subject of our interest and constantly revise it, a rudimentary path gets formed in this green patch of land. With continuous efforts and repetition, the rudimentary path gets converted into strongly cemented roads, and these strongly cemented roads can be referred to as SANSKARs.

Let's take this with another example of your habits: let's assume you have created your Sanskars of always being happy and cheerful, so you on a daily basis intentionally or unintentionally follow this habit of being happy or cheerful, which initially makes these neural networks established in the form of the rudimentary path and with regular practice, these neural networks for happiness feeling will be as strong as cemented roads in our mind. So, whatever happens, you will always be happy in your mind. But certain it takes years of practice to have these kinds of sanskara engrained in your mind.

Similar is the case with negative Sanskars, if you unintentionally practice the feeling of anger, hatred, sense of insecurity or negative feelings or thoughts, your mind will have strong neural networks of these negative feelings cemented, and it would always be hard to avoid these negative feelings of anger, hatred in any kind of circumstances.

What is triggering these Sanskara

The important part to note here is that whether it is good sanskara or bad sanskara, none of them gets to start playing automatically in your mind. There always be an external trigger required to invoke these strong cemented neural networks or Sanskara. These triggers come from 6 forms: 5 external sense organs and 6th one is thoughts in your mind.

How to overcome negative Sanskara (Impressions)

- Don't fear these negative sanskara –Just accept them. Be at peace with them. Fighting with them in your mind will make them more strong.
- Be mindful of them – what is correct and what is not correct?
- Note down the triggers behind the creation of these sanskaras.
- Create positive sanskara by a strong will to replace the negative ones.
- Stop these trigger points by not paying attention to them.[11]

Also, the good news is that all of us are born with an inbuilt pause button, which can be harnessed through practice.

SOUL

7 Innate qualities of Soul: During one of the knowledge and meditation session, I got to understand about these seven innate qualities of Human soul

- Purity: Purity is identified as one of the innate qualities of Soul. When you see a newborn, you can always find

11 https://balakishore.in/articles/neuro-science-behind-sanskar-transformation/

the purity in his eyes; he looks at everyone with the same sense of attachment. All the world belongs to him.

- Bliss: Bliss is the state of complete happiness, joy, fulfilment and satisfaction.
- Knowledge: Knowledge is about seeking the ultimate truth of life, that is your very basic nature.
- Power: Power is the ability to understand what is good for you and society at large
- Peace: Peace is a state of contentment with the situation, people and circumstances around you.
- Happiness: Happiness is a state or feeling of belongingness for all with joy.
- Love: Love is the most fundamental element of mother nature. This feeling drives the world.

Shifting your awareness from Body consciousness to Soul Consciousness

When an individual is living, his life is in 'body consciousness' mode. He always lives by comparing different people, dividing people into good and bad, and is always carried away by the desires (as a slave of desires) and he always has a fear of death.

But when that individual shifts from body consciousness to soul consciousness, he starts accepting people, things, situations as they are, and he has more unity of thoughts and actions, thereby becoming the master of his senses with an elevated awareness of eternity

> If you pray to GOD with all your heart, (dropping the sorrow which simply means hanging onto the past) then whatever you desire will be given to you – Ashtavakra Gita

ANSWERING THE QUESTION: "WHAT IS GOD" – PARMATMA OR SUPREME SOUL

I was reading a book of Swami Vivekananda – one of the greatest mystics, leader and personally the noblest character of modern India. He envisioned so many things and wrote such in-depth words that all his teaching and lectures are still the most relevant for modern India as a subset and of course for a wider world and humanity. When Narendra Nath (later known as Swami Vivekananda) was small, he always had this quest for searching the truth and going beyond the physical boundaries. He was one of the most talented personas.

As he grew up, he always kept asking different people he met: " Have you seen GOD or experienced GOD?". To this, he got a reply from Saint Ramakrishna – one of the greatest devotee of Maa Kaali. He replied, "Yes, I have seen GOD and experienced GOD". As we all know, Swamiji became of his disciples, and the rest is history.

Whenever Saint Ramakrishna Paramahansa used to experience Maa Kaali in the temple, the room or place used to get filled with light all around.

There are multitudes of examples: All realized masters, whenever they have experienced GOD, they experienced it in the form of boundless energy or light.

Humans are considered as Atma, and God is mentioned as "Parmatma- Supreme Soul". With multiple births which Soul takes, original Soul characteristics getting depleted. If we consider souls as batteries, our batteries get discharged over cycles of multiple births, God can be considered as Powerhouse which keeps all the SOULs on this earth charged.

As per ancient Vedic scriptures: Supreme Father or GOD or Parmatma or Supreme Soul has been referred with adjective or name of "Sat-Chit-Ananda" – " Sat – means life" " Chit- Mind or intellect", "Ananda – Pure bliss (indescribable flow of happiness)"

Story of 5 Blind-Folded Persons

Once upon a time, there were five people in the house who were blindfolded. Also, there was one more person along with them-who was able to see everything. This one person knew that there was the elephant in the room, but other five were not aware of it.

All these five blind folded people were asked to describe the elephant, just by touching it

1st person was taken closer to the foot of the elephant, he touched the elephant and told that the elephant was like a "POLE."

2nd person was taken closer to the back of the elephant, he touched and described the elephant as "WALL."

3rd person was taken closer to the ears of the elephant; he considered elephant as "FAN."

4th person was taken closer to the tail of the elephant; he considered elephant as "ROPE."

5th person was taken close to the trunk of the elephant; he experiences elephant as "SNAKE."

When they all were asked to open their blindfold and see it, all of them were amazed and pleasantly shocked to see, what they described or considered an elephant was nowhere near the reality.

We all at the time, with our limited experiences of life, try to describe GOD with our limited vision, but the reality is way beyond that. He is way beyond all of us – limitless, boundless and infinite.

I was attending one of the advance meditation retreats, where one of the teachers asked all the attendees to draw a circle and put the name of the dearest individual, all of them have written their names or friends or family or near or dear one's name, but none of them have written – "GOD" in the circle.

We are children of "GOD" and expect so much from our supreme father, but we don't even bother to consider him in the circle of our dearest. Still "Parmatma" or "supreme father" fulfils all our desires whenever we remember him with purity in heart.

Law of Karma – Balance Sheet of Life

During the battle of Kurukshetra, When Arjuna was feeling helpless, Lord Krishna gave Arjuna the knowledge/Law of Karma. Bhagwat Geeta is more of the dialogue between Lord Krishna -supreme master/Guru and his disciple - Arjuna in the middle of the battlefield. Law of Karma says that we should do our actions honestly considering it as our duties without thinking/worrying about any intent or results or outcome.

All our actions are recorded in the form of the balance sheet of life, whenever we do anything good for others, society, it is more of credit in your account of life. If we plan, plot or do anything wrong with others, it is more of a negative balance or Debit in our life account.

So, we should keep focusing on making positive deposits in our life balance sheet by doing our doing goods, avoid debits from our accounts.

If we always live our life with Karma Philosophy – Balance sheet of life – we become more happy, peaceful and contented in life.

We can correlate this with this simple example: someone gets birth in a very rich and wealthy family, others get born in a middle-class family and someone in a low-income family. This can be explained from the concept of past karmas – balance sheet of life which have an impact on you.

WHY SHOULD I BE GOOD WHEN PEOPLE AROUND ME ARE MEAN

I got a chance to interact with EV Swami sir during one of the advance knowledge sessions. I happened to ask this question with him: why should we be good when people all around me are "MEAN". If we see at a superficial level about life, we see MEAN people at times are wealthy and living a great life. He replied with a story. Here goes the story. Swami sir, out of his passion for contributing back to society, used to conduct sessions for small kids in the age group of 8-13 years. These years are the most formative years for children since he/she enters the teenage during this time. If life is understood correctly by the young blood, it can completely change the course of life for them. During the summer camp, there was a girl called Ananya around 10-11 years. Swami sir used to always say to all his students, be nice to your family, listen to what your mom, dad says, always obey them. Always respect their words.

He said the same thing to this girl Ananya. She had the profound influence of Swami sir, so she thought of following his teachings. Whenever she used to go home, she used to more polite and humble and used to hear what her mom used to offer, used to study on time, sleep on time, food on time. She stopped being adamant about her demands with her mom. Suddenly her parents found this drastic positive change in Ananya's behaviour and asked her about it. She told them that she had been following what Swami sir had taught her. Parents thanked Swami sir for bringing so much positive change in the life of this little girl. It was all going fine. One day Swami sir saw Ananya a bit sad and annoyed, he asked her "Why are you feeling so sad"?

Instead you should be feeling happy since your parents see you as a transformed child". To this question, Ananya replied "What is the benefit of me being a good child – I am doing all that my parents are asking me to do, I obey them completely, whenever I want to do anything which is not according to their wishes, I remember your words and stop arguing with them. I don't over-power them anymore, and I do what they want me to do. But what is the benefit for me in this". She started sobbing and told, "Sir It was great before when I used to argue with my parents, used to demand the things which I wanted, used to get the things done as per my wishes. But now I am not getting any of it. I am more on the losing side by obeying to my parents, and I am not getting benefitted out of it. It was better earlier: when I was a mean child, at least my wishes were getting completed on time. Now I have to crush my wishes inside". This small question of a little girl "WHY SHOULD I be good in this mean world" left swami sir thinking all night. Next day, Swami sir went again to Ananya. He told her – "Yes visibly it looks like you are losing out by not getting what you demanded from your parents, looks like your wishes are not getting fulfilled, but if you think deeper, with the sacrifices of these small things, don't you think – you are getting the most precious of all things – More love, more attention, more quality time, sense of responsibility from your parents – indeed it is like an **invisible currency** of trust, faith, obedient child, great character building for future getting deposited in your life account in return of the petty visible loss of your earlier wishes." Ananya immediately understood this concept of deposits of invisible currencies of goodness being accumulated in individual life.

After hearing this story of Ananya, I got my answer to "Why should I be good to others when people around me are MEAN"?

Marshmallow experiment and Power of Delayed Gratification[12]

There was an experiment carried out an initial set of 32 children – 16 boys and 16 girls in 1972 by leading psychologist Walter Mischel – a professor at Stanford University for studying the subject of delayed gratification. It was called the Marshmallow

12 https://en.wikipedia.org/wiki/Stanford_marshmallow_experiment

experiment. The children were in the age range of 3 years and six months to 5years and eight months. As part of this experiment, a child was offered with the choice of selecting between one small but immediate reward or two rewards if they waited for some period. The researcher left the room with a marshmallow on the table near the child and returned after 15 mins. In the follow-up study, researchers found that children who were able to wait for 15 mins and were able to resist the temptation had better life outcomes as measured by SAT scores.

This experiment is still relevant for recent times as well. Individuals who have a sense of delaying the gratification for a more extended period and able to resist back temptations of life would be more contented with an overall perspective of life.

TIME BEING ETERNAL ELEMENT - KAAL CHAKRA – SCIENTIFIC EXPLANATION (FROM ENTROPY 0 TO 1)

The intent of the discussion pointer on Time is, it is the most powerful of all and how we can analyze it from a spiritual and scientific viewpoint. Time is the most fundamental of all the elements of nature. It is always changing and cyclical. As the earth rotates on its axis in 24 hours, it brings days and night to this world. Earth completes its revolution around the Sun in 365 and ¼ days, with this revolution, it brings different seasons on this planet earth – Summer, Winter, Rainy, Spring, Autumn.

During one of the advance knowledge and meditation sessions with Brahma Kumaris, I got to know about these deep secrets of the earth cycle – Kaal Chakra. One full cycle of **Yuga is called Kalpa**. Kalpa is usually 5000 years. This is called Eternal time cycle. Our mother earth has undergone multiple cycles, rounds and iterations of YUGAs/KALPA. This time duration of 5000 years is divided into four ages or Yuga. This sounded utterly logical to me as nature of time is always cyclical, resulting into day and nights, different season and different YUGAs.

Each Yuga or Age is hypothetical of 1250 years duration, is cyclical and repetitive

- Golden Age (Satyuga): Age of health, wealth and happiness: 100% Pure Soul: SatoPradhan
- Silver Age (Treta Yuga): Age of gradual decline: Soul quality is still of Sato
- Copper Age (Dwapar Yuga): Age of Bhakti: Soul quality is of Rajo Pradhan
- Iron Age (Kaliyuga): Age of impurity: Soul quality is of Tamo Pradhan: There is a confluence again during the end of Kaliyuga to entry the soul quality back.

As the time cycle elapsed, humans moved from the Soul consciousness state to body consciousness state. During Golden (Satyuga) and Silver (TretraYuga) age, the human was still predominantly into Soul consciousness state, During the last two age – Copper (Dwapar) and Iron Age (Kaliyuga), Soul got completed degraded to Body consciousness state.

This overall duration of 5000 years called Kaal Chakra can also be understood from the scientific concept of Entropy.

Entropy (E) is defined as the measurement of the degree of randomness of the energy in the system, so it means if the system is highly random or least ordered in nature, then it has the highest entropy of 1 and if the system is least random or highly ordered then the entry of the system is Zero.

The entropy of any of the system varies between 0 to 1. So we apply this scientific understanding of Entropy to the Energy system of Earth during different Yuga (age), we can establish that during Satyuga, the world was perfectly in order, so the entropy (E)during that time frame of initial 1250 years was Zero, as time elapsed, a stable system moves from stability to randomness by its nature, so is the case of Yuga (age), as time elapsed from Satyuga to Treta Yuga, entropy (randomness of energy increased) from zero to some hypothetic positive value (say .25) during the next age 1250 years to 2500 years.

Again, after the end of Treta Yuga and starting of Dvapara Yuga, overall random increased to more positive value hypothetically (say .5).

Again, after the end of Dwapar Yuga to starting to Kaliyuga, overall randomness and value of entropy further increased to (say .75)

In Kaliyuga, entropy is highest in terms of reaching it closer to 1 (E = 1), which is the highest state of randomness, so if we need to move back from the state of highest randomness (E=1) to the state of lowest randomness (E=0), external stimulus/energy is required to restore the order in soul.

So, in this extreme state of randomness, Meditation is the only tool which provides the stimulus for this SOUL to help connect it back to SUPREME SOUL.

PART 4

TRANSFORMING LIVES AROUND THE WORLD

Each one of you is a light house of happiness...!!!
See how you can be useful to people around you…!!!
– GURUDEV SRI SRI

During my journey as sincere seeker trying to find the answers of few of the life questions, I realized that although it is essential to understand the answers of these questions: "WHO AM I", "What is GOD", " WHY SHOULD I BE GOOD IN THIS MEAN WORLD", but surely this is not the purpose of life and existence, since there are millions who are living in this world without knowing the answers of these questions and as I went more in-depth in my quest for the meaning of life, I was utterly convinced that the aim is to serve the society at large and bring transformation around the world by making it a happier place to live. By focus on this broader purpose of life, you will not only be able to get connected to yourself but also the supreme soul.

STRESS – THE SILENT KILLER

Stress is the biggest silent killer leading to the death of people across the globe. According to one of the reports of WHO: top 10 causes of death accounts for more than 54% of deaths worldwide (56.9 Million deaths in 2016)[13]. As per the American

13 https://www.who.int/news-room/fact-sheets/detail/the-top-10-causes-of-death

Psychological Association, chronic stress is linked to the six leading causes of death: heart disease, cancer, lung ailments, accidents, cirrhosis of the liver and suicide

Top 10 global causes of deaths, 2016

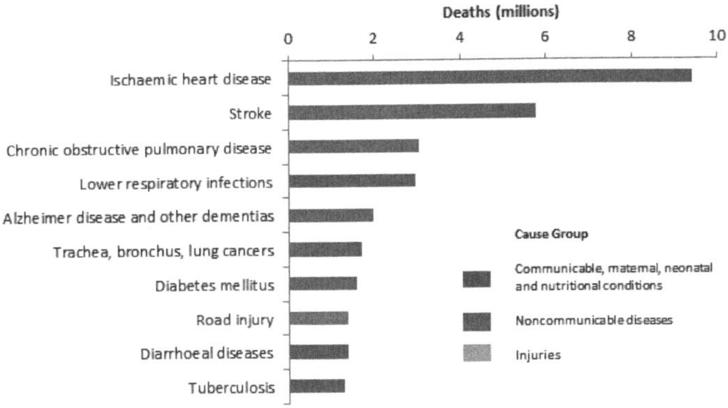

Source: Global Health Estimates 2016: Deaths by Cause, Age, Sex, by Country and by Region, 2000-2016. Geneva, World Health Organization; 2018.

Top 10 causes of deaths in upper-middle-income countries in 2016

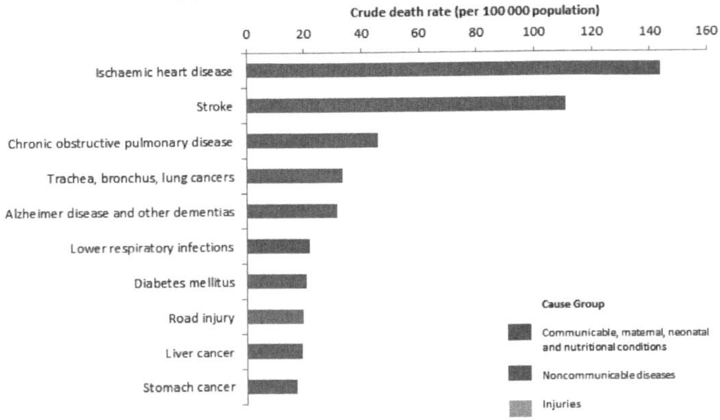

Source: Global Health Estimates 2016: Deaths by Cause, Age, Sex, by Country and by Region, 2000-2016. Geneva, World Health Organization; 2018.
World Bank list of economies (June 2017). Washington, DC: The World Bank Group; 2017 (https://datahelpdesk.worldbank.org/knowledgebase/articles/906519-world-bank-country-and-lending-groups).

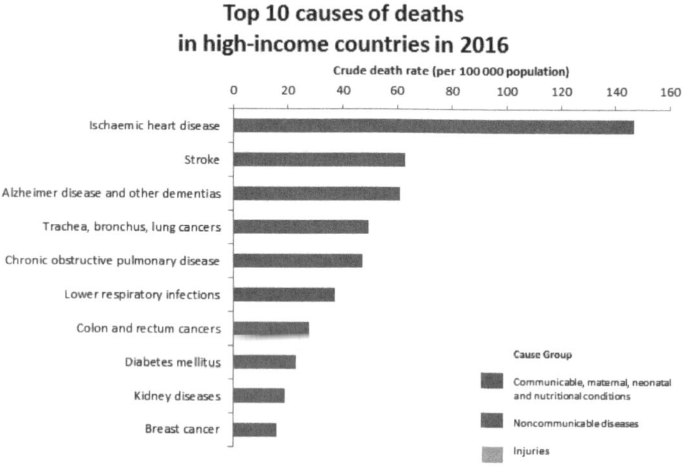

Source: Global Health Estimates 2016: Deaths by Cause, Age, Sex, by Country and by Region, 2000-2016. Geneva, World Health Organization; 2018.
World Bank list of economies (June 2017). Washington, DC: The World Bank Group; 2017 (https://datahelpdesk.worldbank.org/knowledgebase/articles/906519-world-bank-country-and-lending-groups).

CHALLENGES ASSOCIATED WITH THE PROBLEM: STRESS

- Economic Challenges
  - Due to the chronic stress among people in the society: it is resulting into early ageing of the people, and it also results into people suffering from multiple diseases such as heart attack, stroke etc., which affects the earning capacity of the family and society at large and also results into higher money outflow for treatment of these diseases and even at a time resulting in the death of millions of individuals.
- Social Challenges
  - Countries which are under-developed or developing: Stress problem is posing more significant social challenges in society. Developing Countries aimed at spending their limited resources into developing basic infrastructural need to now

focus on enhancing healthcare facilities to cater to diseases resulting from stress. There are no policies in place to address these fundamental issues.

Stress is the gravest concern across the world, resulting in multiple diseases.

While researching on this topic, I got to find some alarming data about Great Britain and Stress – How grave is the situation there and why is it happening. Here are the statistics from the survey results conducted by a firm [14] . I am sure even for other countries (including India), figures will be equally alarming as well.

- 85% of UK adults are experiencing stress regularly
- Over a third of British residents feel stressed for at least one full day a week
- The most common causes for stress are money, work and health concerns, failure to get enough sleep and household chores
- 39% of UK adults admit they felt too stressed in their day to day lives
- 54% of people who are stressed worry about the impact, it has on their health
- Women suffer from stress for three more days per month than men

On the similar lines below are the major sources of stress for American adults[15]

14 www.forthwithlife.co.uk

15 https://www.stress.org/workplace-stress

Main Causes of Stress

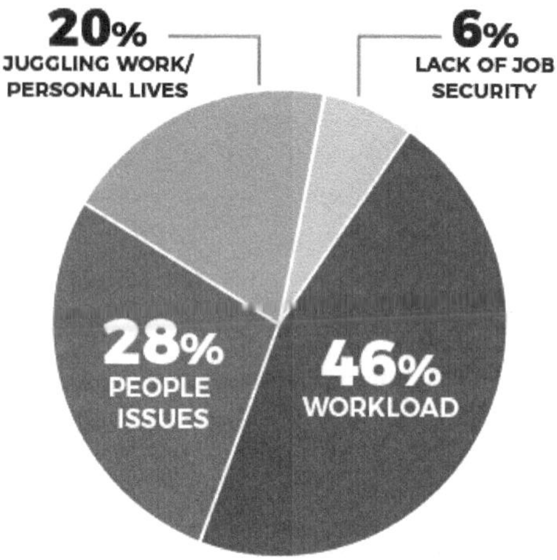

Source: EAP provider ComPsych's first half of 2006 StressPulse Survey.

HOW TO HANDLE THE PROBLEM OF STRESS

This is a huge problem not just for the developed world, but also for people in developing and under-developed countries, but certainly, there is way out for tackling it at every level. Spirituality is the solution for this problem by making the individual understand the connection with himself – spirit or Soul.

It can be tackled at different levels by creating awareness at:

- Individual-level
- Leadership level
- Corporate or Enterprise level
- Different societies level
- Different countries and government level
- Global Citizens level

INDIVIDUAL-LEVEL

In this digital world, we need to understand the importance of Digital well-being for individuals

Bringing Digital well-being and transformation for individuals in this world

I got the chance to attend a 'Thought Management and Leadership' workshop organized by Jaipur Engineering College and Research Center. During this three day workshop, I heard from Mr Balakishore – VP Transformation Search Software on the topic of Digital Wellness. I was incredibly impressed by his thought process and a deep understanding of the concept of Digital wellness and overall Human well-being.

Mobile phone these days have been the most powerful piece of technology, but sadly they are silently making us their slaves as well – we all have now got addicted so much to our mobile phones that we can live without our families for a couple of days or couple of months, but certainly can't live without a mobile phone even without an hour altogether. Way back in the early days of 2007 or before when there was hardly any smart-phone penetration in this world, the world was still living on feature phones, and NOKIA was still the kings of MOBILE phone. I have nothing against smartphones, but certainly these smartphones, in addition to making us smart by bringing all the information at our fingertips, have also created so much digital toxicity and addictions among humans. The truth is, when a child is hardly few months old, we as parents expose them to smartphones for making them learn phonics or songs or nursery rhymes, and in no time, it impacts these little ones to such an extent that, we don't see the boundaries between the gadgets and gadgets becomes our life.

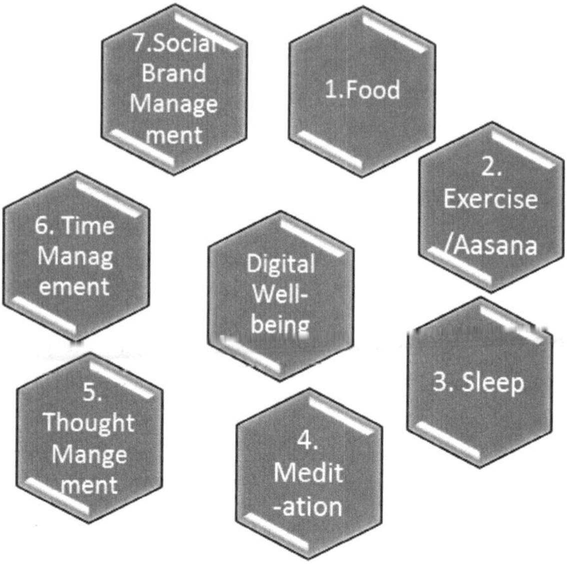

- **Food**: Food has the biggest impact on human being. Whatever we consume, it gets accumulated in the form of our body. When we are there in our mother's womb for nine months, we get food from her, and we grow – 3 to 4 Kg at the time of birth, subsequently from 4Kg at the time of birth to 70 to 80 Kg, we grow so much by the food we consume. It is always advised to eat Sattvic food, rather than Rajasic or Tamasic food as there is a direct correlation between the kind of food you eat and the thoughts which comes in your mind. Sattvic food includes seasonal foods and fruits benefitting your body. Sattvic food improves the qualities of Sattva – pureness, true, honesty, ahimsa. Consuming Sattvic food maintain the required energy level needed for the day-to-day functioning of the body. Consuming Tamasic food decreases the overall Prana or energy level in the body. Tamasic food brings lethargy and obesity to the human body.

Rajasic food brings a sudden increase in the energy level in the body and hence more anger in humans. It is always advised to have vegetarian food or Sattvic food since if we see our human body, our body is designed to eat vegetarian food. If we observe the structure of teeth in our mouth: We have Incisors, Canines, Premolars and Molars. Humans hardly have well-developed incisors or canines; we have more number and greater developed premolar and molar teeth.

If we also closely observe: flesh-eating or wild animals, they have well-developed canines or incisor to tear the flesh of the body. On the other hand, our teeth or jaw structure is most conducive and like domestic animals which usually feeds on Vegetarian food.

Our structure of alimentary canal - including the mouth, pharynx, esophagus, stomach, and intestine, anus (food inlet to removing waste from the body) is very conducive for digestion of vegetarian food as it gets digested in 8 to 10 hours times.

If we eat meat or non-vegetarian food, it takes more than 24 to 48 hours getting digested in our body, which results in some undigested food lying on the walls of the intestine and getting fermented, causing issues with our overall digestive system

- **Exercise/ Asanas /Body Postures**: I cannot over-emphasize on the importance of exercise on our body. We need to cultivate the habit of spending at least 30 mins on the overall well-being of our body – starting from our head, neck, shoulder, upper body, lower body, legs, hips till the toes. We should carry our body rotation for these. Surya-Namaskar is a great set of Yoga asana meant for different body parts. If we get bored doing the same set of exercise or Asanas every day, include new or different yoga postures conducive to the body structure. Never over-do anything

Benefits of physical exercise

- Promotes Brain health
- Increases the rate of the overall learning
- Reduces anxiety and stress
- Reduces the risk of heart attack, diabetes, colon cancer, high BP
- Builds Bones, Muscles and Joints
- Improves Immune System
- Most effective Happiness booster

- **Sleep.** Sleep is the most relaxing moment and helps you heal your body. We need to have proper sleep time and habit; this also improves our immunity and digestive system as well. Most of the time, whenever we go to bed for sleeping, we still watch our mobile messages, emails or browse applications, which is not good for a sound sleep. We need to mentally prepare our mind on a daily basis to be devoid any distractions before our sleep. Hence avoid watching mobile just before sleep.

  Quick tips to sleep well:

  - Don't use the mobile phone at least for an hour before your sleep time
  - Don't exercise too late in the evening
  - Avoid taking large meals and beverages late in the night
  - Have a clutter-free environment for good sleep, meaning your bed and bed stool area should be in proper order and arranged in a neat and tidy manner. Place for every item and all items in place.
  - Have right sunlight exposure during the day

While researching on this topic, I got to understand some interesting facts as collated by Bala Kishore Ji [16]and Bramham Kumaris. I am sharing some insights on the same below.

16 https://balakishore.in/digital-wellness/

Impact of Sleep loss on Heart (High risk of Heart Attack – due to calcification of coronary arteries)

- There are more than twenty large-scale epidemiological studies that have tracked millions of people over many decades, all of which report the same clear relationship: the shorter your sleep, the shorter your life.
- People who sleep for 6 hours or less than 6 hours daily have **45% more risk** of developing Heart Diseases
- Adults who are forty-five years or older who sleep fewer than 6 hours a night are **200 per cent** more likely to have a heart attack or stroke during their lifetime, as compared with those sleeping seven to eight hours a night

Impact of Sleep loss on Diabetes and obesity

- Individuals sleeping less than 6 hours on a daily basis have a higher risk of developing Diabetes
- Sleep deprivation increases Insulin-Resistance thus increasing sugar levels in the blood
- Chronic Sleep deprivation decreases the activity of Leptin hormone & increases the activity of Ghrelin hormone
- Leptin hormone signals 'fullness', Ghrelin hormone signals 'hunger.'
- Dieting without proper Sleep burns muscle mass, not fat
- The sleep-deprived body will cry famine during plenty

Impact of Sleep loss on immunity (Reduction of Immunity)

- Adequate Sleep restores Immune System activity and helps individual fight Infections in a better manner
- Sleep Loss reduces Immunity and makes the person more susceptible to Infections

- Sleep Loss also increases inflammation inside the body and contributes to the development of Cancerous cells
- When an individual falls sick, our Immune System activates Sleep System for better recovery[17]

Impact of Sleep loss leading to ALZHEIMER'S

- Higher levels of Beta-amyloid plaque observed in the brains of Alzheimer's patients
- Good Night Sleep found to help cleanup beta-amyloid plaque
- Alzheimer's especially erodes NREM sleep

Getting too little sleep across the adult life span will significantly raise your risk of developing Alzheimer's disease

Below are the details of sleep requirements for different groups of people based on the study done by (Source: National Sleep Foundation[18])

17 Matthew Walker. "Why We Sleep: Unlocking the Power of Sleep and Dreams

18 National Sleep foundation

Sleep the greatest gift of mother nature to all living beings

If we deeply analyze, after 'breathing', our 'sleep' is the next most essential element for life. As Breathing is critical for living, so is sleep essential for overall well-being. Sleep helps slow down our overall mental activity. Sleep is like you keeping your computer or laptop in shut-down mode to avoid draining of battery or wastage of power. Also, if we observe closely, our ideal mind thinking patterns or behaviour during the sleep and the quantity of thoughts gets reduced, and the quality improves.

Also, if you observe, a good sleep pattern at night helps in better digestion of food. Sleep acts as a reboot button for human machines and helps them to heal body organs by themselves. Yogic sleep is considered as the best sleep, wherein mind activity or thoughts become minimal, and the body goes in the complete state of rest resulting in maximum healing of the body by utilizing the energy properly

During a study in the late 1960s, two scientists, Rechtschaffen and Kales, defined a typical sleep cycle, displaying the varying levels of consciousness. A complete cycle lasts around 90 to 110 minutes. In their studies, it shows Sleep consists of four stages - Stage 1, Stage2, Stage3 and Stage4.

Stage 4 being the closest to Deep sleep state. So during a typical sleep duration of 8-9 hours at night, human mind hardly reaches Stage 4 if you are very active just before your sleeping time. The more we get ourselves relaxed or meditate before sleeping, the likelihood of reaching Stage 4 -Deep Sleep increases tremendously.

Also, as we see the deep-rooted connection between your mind, thoughts and sleep, if anyone needs to improve his sleep pattern, he needs to start instructing and mentally preparing the mind for this, so that overall sleep quality improves.

As per scientific experiments on the brain, if we observe the **electroencephalogram** (EEG) with overall Brain states and activities, we can find EEG pattern can be majorly categorized into five states as per their frequencies:

- Gamma State – Hyperactive state (30- 40 Hz)
- Beta State – Alert state (13 to 30 Hz)
- Alpha State – Sub Mind State (8-12 Hz)
- Theta state – Relaxed state (4 – 8 Hz)
- Delta State – Rest state/ Deep Sleep (.5 – 4 Hz)

So, when we meditate regularly, we can achieve Theta state of mind very often and which over the period, also helps us to improve our overall quality of sleep as well.

So with current life-style which all of us possess, our mind hardly reaches Theta or Delta state during the sleep at night, most of the time, whatever actions we take during the day, keep replaying back in the night resulting in degradation of overall quality of sleep at night.

It is not only adults who are facing the problems of insomnia or sleeplessness, but even children have also started facing these problems due to the kind of content being fed to their brain via TV or mobile or other daily activities as part of their surroundings.

- **Meditation**: if Yoga asanas are exercise for your body, meditation is an exercise for your mind and soul. It helps you to bring back the balance of life. We can spend at least 10-15 mins daily on meditation. You can use different methods of meditations – Guided Meditation, Chanting, meditating through light music, etc.

- **Thought Management**: if we manage all the earlier elements of Digital wellness such as food, exercise, sleep, meditation into the systematic way, then automatically your thought management improves and you start to have more positive thoughts and avoid any negative or waste thoughts.

- **Time Management**: In order to carry out all these activities mentioned above, we need to manage our time in the best possible manner. It is always advised to follow: Time management Matrix. I got to read about it – Time Management Matrix in – The seven habits of highly effective people. The first step is analyzing your daily routine for the last couple of weeks and try to list down all the major tasks, activities, time duration for the same. Once you have the list of activities based on the daily routine which you have been following-up during the last couple of weeks or months. Now try to categorize them into these four quadrants:
    - **Q1 (Urgent and important):** Focus on the 1st as they are an immediate attention seeker. Ideally, there should be lesser and lesser activities in the quadrant. This is like living in a fire-fighting mode every day if we have lots of item in 1st quadrant. It is also indicative of the fact that we are not able to manage our life well, resulting in everything falling as a matter of urgency and importance. We need to make sure that our 1st quadrant is the least cluttered to make our life smooth sailing.
    - **Q2 (Not Urgent and Important):** Ideally we should always be focusing our quality time on this quadrant, as it is related to your current tasks or capabilities which if you can focus will always make you future-ready. Also, you should plan your Q2 quadrant well, to avoid slipping activities from Q2 to Q1. If you don't pay complete attention to Q2, then there are chances you are going to run out of time shortly and will be in firefighting mode. All successful people always focus most of their time on Q2 and plan their day to address activities in Q2. Managing Q2 Quadrant is the key to success.

- **Q3 (Urgent and not Important):** Activities in Q3 is something which is always unplanned and falls from the blue, we have not anticipated these activities, and neither has planned our time for it. But as a matter of urgency needs to be worked upon priorities.

  Let's assume you are doing your work and suddenly your boss calls you and ask you to complete one report for him urgently. These kinds of tasks at a time falls under this quadrant, which can result in stress at times if not handled properly. Also, these activities need to handle asap and cannot be delayed or eliminated. We should plan our day anticipating 10-15% of tasks might come-up via Q3 route, so we should be mentally prepared to have them to avoid any kind of stress. If we are prepared for these kinds of unplanned – urgent tasks, then we can give our best to complete them.

- **Q4 (Not urgent and not important):** we need to ensure that activities in this quadrant are eliminated completely as they are a waste of time and energy. They produce wasteful or negative thoughts, resulting in draining of our energies.

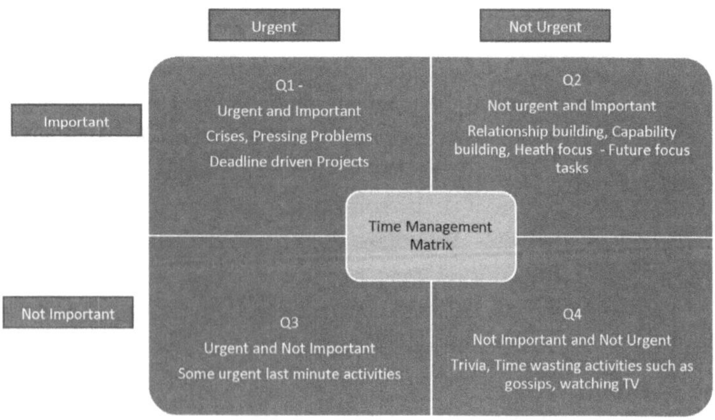

- **Social Brand Management**: It is always important to think about all individuals as social brands. We play different roles in a single day – a father, a husband, a brother, a boss, a team player, a social worker – for playing these different roles, we need to have different kinds of egos or masks, so that we can do our work effectively. So, if we see what overall social brand value is: it is a reflection of your work as perceived by others. Maybe you are a terrible husband, but can be a great father, good brother, great boss or average team player. We certainly need to have very strong emotional quotient & intelligence to manage them all well. I can certainly say with complete honesty that we can't be a superhero in all the roles which we play every day, and it is natural to be like that. Most important is doing our tasks honestly in the role which we are playing. We should constantly ask these two questions to ourselves:
    - What kind of a person do you want to be?
    - What kind of a world, do you want to create for yourself to live in?

And we should always try to give our best since there is no competition with others, but certainly a commitment to the self to be a better version of yourself every day passing by. The most important thing to be done right now on this planet is to raise human consciousness. Every human should have an elevated view of life. Meditation helps us to achieve the same. One thought which we should always wake up to in the morning is to create a loving world around us.

LEADERSHIP LEVEL

Bringing transformation at the leadership level

Leadership is the most talked about and searched topic on Google. In the simplest words: leadership is the ability to influence people and bringing out the best from people in all kind of situations. You need to have an impact on the behaviour, attitudes, opinions and choices of others. When a leader is leading, he needs to influence, establish credibility, engage with others and build a connection, clarify expectations and practice accountability. He needs to share your passion and should be ready to be in your shoes to understand.

In both categories: we can have two types of leaderships:

- **Positional leadership**: In case of positional leadership, people or team will follow or respect you, due to the position which you hold. Since you are upholding the forte or position, it is usually short-lived. Once the leader leaves that position, people may or may not follow them. This leadership style works well when the knowledge or skills of your team is lesser than you. A typical example of manufacturing step-up where in shop floor worker will hear to his supervisor or advisor for day-today operational work
- **Influential leadership**: In case of knowledge economy wherein everyone is at par with you in terms of skills or knowledge, then Positional leadership might not work, in such scenarios, influential leadership is the key to success.

  In the book: *The Secret: What Great Leaders Know and Do*, Ken Blanchard and Mark Miller provide in-depth SERVE Model of leadership:

  - S: See the future
  - E: Engage and develop the team
  - R: Reinvent continuously

- V: Value your results and relationship
- E: Embody the values which you promulgate

A great leader has a serving heart which beats for both organization and team. Nelson Mandel, Dr Kalaam were few of the examples of influential leadership style.

I got a chance to attend one of the leadership summits, wherein I heard the thoughts of Sneh Desai – Expert motivator and inspirational coach. I completely echo his views on leadership and non-leadership traits of individuals.

Below are the few non-leadership traits, which are completely a NO NO and hence needs to be avoided at every cost:

- **Fear and Insecurity**: Every human has his/her sense of worries and insecurities, and as individuals reach the top leadership position, chances of these insecurities and fears increasing are higher, as there is so much cut-throat competition always to deliver results. In these kinds of circumstances, it is more important to have a deep understanding of "SELF – 7 innates qualities" which we discussed earlier. With the realization of self, it brings more clarity in thought process and removes these negative thoughts and tendencies of – Fear and Insecurity.
- **"I want it now" Shortcut Attitudes**: Individuals tend to have attitudes of shortcut in life. But certainly, life doesn't offer any short cuts to success. You certainly need to have the skills required to be successful. 'I want it now' attitude does not work most of the time since this impulsive behaviour does not lead to collaborative behaviour among individuals. If we see the examples of all long-term successful leaders – all of them have gone through their journeys of life to achieve those successes. There is a difference between SMART working and short-cut; both should not be considered the same. SMART working helps in cutting short some of the time, but it not a short cut. Thomas Edison – one

of the American greatest inventors and businessman of 19th centuries have the following life quotes:

- *Genius is one per cent inspiration and ninety-nine per cent perspiration.*
- *I have not failed. I've just found 10,000 ways that won't work.*
- *Our greatest weakness lies in giving up. The most certain way to succeed is always to try just one more time.*

- **Blame Game**: Most of the time we see when there is any success, leaders take credit of those successes and in case of any failures, blame game begins aimed at pointing fingers at each other and trying to fix blame on others for their failure. This attitude certainly needs to be avoided. We certainly need to take complete responsibilities of ours and our teams' actions.

  DR APJ Kalam is a great leader to be followed in this kind of scenarios. Here is one story of Dr Kalam sir's life. In 1979, he was leading the SLV-3 space mission, and the project failed. Professor Satish Dhawan, who was the chairman of ISRO, then comforted his team. Later at the press conference, ISRO chief Satish Dhawan sir informed the nation of the failure and took all the blame upon himself in front of everyone. Dr Kalam quoted, I learned an important lesson and the best management experience that day. When failure occurred, the leader of the organization owned that failure. When success came, Satish Dhawan asked Dr Kalam to go and attend the press conference and gave credit to the team.

  As an organizational and personal leadership, we need to avoid the attitude of BLAME-GAME in the team.

- **Hopelessness**: There are certain leaders who always are pessimistic about any situation or scenarios of life. Thoughts of Hopelessness should always be avoided at any cost. It is considered a negative leadership trait. Hope has the power to transform the world. People of Japan are the ones who always lived their lives on Hope. Struck by Atom Bomb on Hiroshima and Nagasaki, killing thousands of people and leaving thousands disabled for life, Japanese rebuilt their nation on new hope of life, and within no-time, Japan becomes world number 2 economy. During the 1980s, Japanese companies such as Toyota, Honda, Suzuki revamped the automobile market and started exporting their products to the American market and became a hallmark of success.

- **Life Imbalance**: Life is all about maintaining the balance between work and personal life. One of the non-leadership traits is giving all attention to work at the cost of family time, resulting in Life imbalance. There are multiple examples of leaders in organizations which gives their 100% focus on the work and feel proud about this and expect the team to have similar behaviour. These kinds of situations can be taken as an exception in case of any crisis situations, but certainly, it can't be considered as normal work routine.

- **Self-obsessed or Being no. 1**: Individuals want to be no. 1 at any cost, and leaders are so self-obsessed in achieving their targets that they are willing to let go of morality at times. There is a very thin line between being ambitious and being obsessed towards success at any cost.

- **Listen to me**: In some of the organizations, there is an authoritative style of management wherein leaders call out that 'listen to me and follow it'. But if we closely observe, successful leadership is more collaborative in approach, and the decision making is done through consensus mechanism rather than 'listen to me' approach

- **My way or the highway**: Respecting the differences of opinion is a sign of strong leadership rather than weakness. Most of the time, when there is an authoritative leader who is driving a change gives a mandate that, 'either my way or the highway', it looks like he or she can drive the change successfully in short term frame. But in the long term, this attitude results in a deep organizational loss in the form of core people leaving the organization. Respecting other views and being more collective and collaborative always yields long term sustainable results.

Great Leaders possess the following key traits:

- **Be a lifelong learner**: Great leaders always have an attitude of lifelong learners and are always open to discussions. They know that a leader doesn't know each and everything, and he must play as more of a facilitator and navigator through the tough times. The attitude of lifelong learner helps to handle tough or uncertain situations with a more positive approach, rather than succumb to it. In any kind of scenarios, decisions are made based on the available data, knowledge of past situations and considering future vision. Lifelong learner approach helps you to be very flexible and adaptive in your approach during changing circumstances around you.

  Characteristics of lifelong learners:

  - Open-minded / flexible in their approach
  - Believe in sharing knowledge and skills
  - Stay curious
  - Seek resources
  - Develop good reading habits
  - Set goals for learnings
  - Great collaborators
  - I was a student; I am a student, and I will be a student

- **Self-Awareness:** Self Awareness is the greatest leadership trait. If you can control your body, minds and thoughts, you are always in full control of any kind of situation around you, whether pleasant or unpleasant. We all have an in-built PAUSE button which helps us to decide our response to the situations around us. Power of self-awareness provides us with the freedom to choose the correct response in the toughest of all situations. Traits of Self-awareness can be created through the practice of mindfulness which gives you complete control of life.

- **Start with a definite end:** All of us are born with the habits of procrastination. Difference between good and a great leader is, a great leader always starts any task with a definite end in mind. They visualize the future in their mind and then work towards achieving it. So, things get created twice in this world, once in your visualization and then in actuals. Starting with a definite end helps a person to always deliver the results well within the time. It also ensures that the leader and team do the planning of the activities and resources based on that. Most of the sports personnel and Olympic athletes clearly visualize the end state in their mind of the events and then follow the discipline to walk the path for achieving it. Visualization is an important step, but certainly working towards achieving is equally important to achieve it.

- **Set your priorities**: Setting up the priorities helps you to be more focused in your approach towards any task. Every individual has multiple commitments and tasks to complete. If the work which you plan to achieve is not a part of your priority list, you will not give quality time for planning or achieving it. After setting up your priorities for the day, giving your quality time is required for successful completion of the task. Let's understand it with an example: I have set up a priority for finishing my book and getting it published in another two months. Once you set this as your priority, then you plan your complete life or work based on that. Finishing the writing piece, Choosing the publisher, getting the content to proofread, planning out your launch and promotion, spreading through word of mouth and finally seeing it happening on the D day of the launch. These are the few steps which are part of your "Book Launch". Each of these needs to be worked upon and planned to achieve your goal of publishing a book within a specific time period.

This concept can be worked upon for any of your priorities in life – whether personal or professional. Setting priorities helps you to clear the cluttered path on the way of achieving your priorities

- **Win-Win Attitude**: Usually individuals have the attitude of "I win, you lose" or "Winners take it all" in any kind of engagement, but certainly the best outcome of any work or engagement is " WIN-WIN attitude". Win-win attitude brings more maturity to the relationship and takes it to the next level. It is also an attitude of the abundance mentality where we believe that nature or mother earth has so much to offer all of us, and we all can live in harmony fulfilling our aspirations and dreams. It shows integrity in our behaviour towards others.

  In this current hyper-competitive world as well, paradigms of business are now focusing on win-win attitude, so that both the parties become partners in each other's success.

  Let's understand this with an example of AUTO industries: In the auto industry, if you plan to make a car, you might be requiring assembling of 100's of auto components and you as an organization cannot manufacture all these components. The best way is to get these components from your 3rd party suppliers at the time when you need them, so you create the ecosystem of collaboration and coexistence so that you can deliver the end product which is "CAR" in this case. All these 3rd party vendors act as your strategic partners for making you successful.

There are similar examples of WIN-WIN relationship in other industries as well; various organizations in the software industry collaborate and cooperate to deliver their products and services to end customers.

- **Emotional Bank Account**: I was reading the book: "The seven habits of highly effective people" by Stephen Covey – in which I got to read about this emotional bank account and concept of major deposits. Whenever we do something good for others, it is considered as "major deposits" for them in the relationship. We need to consciously focus on making regular deposits to the emotional bank accounts of others in any relationship for long term benefits.

  Effective leaders make this a regular practice to invest in their people by making regular deposits in their relationships with them.

  Few actions which can leads to major deposits in any kind of relationships are

  - Understanding the individuals
  - Taking time out for them and listening to them
  - Attending little things
  - Keeping promises and commitments
  - Clarifying expectations
  - Apologizing sincerely whenever you have made any mistakes
  - Never Criticizing

- Giving honest and sincere appreciations
- Giving unconditional love

we should avoid doing major withdraws from the relationships. Few actions which can lead to major withdrawals in relationships are

- Criticizing the people
- Blame-game
- Unrealistic expectations
- Being bossy with people

- **Be a good listener**: God has given us two ears and one mouth to ensure that we listen more than we talk. There can be different levels of listening:

    - Ignoring: not listening at all
    - Pretend to listen: Don't like their views but still forced to listen to them; hence you pretend to listen to them by nodding
    - Selective listening: Listen to only things which matters to you the most and are relevant to you.
    - Attentive listening: when you listen actively to others and ask questions to clarify if anything not understood
    - Empathetic listening: is the most powerful of all listening skills, in which you deeply listen to the person and feel what he/she wants to convey

If you want to be a great listener, then you need to be empathetic in your listening skills to get the rapport established between you and the speaker.

- **Team synergy:** Any effective leader believes in team synergy to achieve the maximum from the given circumstances. He builds synergies by

    - Valuing the difference
    - Building on each other's' strengths
    - Compensating for others' weakness

Team synergies are simple to build by following these magical phrases whenever it is required

- I am wrong
- I am sorry
- You can do it
- I believe in you
- I am proud of you
- Thank you
- I need you
- I trust you
- I respect you

These simple but magical phrases help in creating better bonding with people or team members and motivates them to deliver their best in time of real needs.

Also, when we are talking about team synergy, it is also reflective of synergy within you as an individual. An individual is also like a team – his body, mind, thoughts, energy, emotions, attitude. All of them needs to be aligned for achieving a goal.

Practising Yoga and meditation on a daily basis helps in cultivating greater leadership skills since individual starts rising above self and starts taking wider responsibility for life in and around self. Individuals feel more empowered to his actions and work with a greater focus for overall well-being.

CORPORATE AND ENTERPRISE LEVEL

Bringing transformation in the corporate world[19]

I have been working in the corporate world for more than 15 years, and I certainly feel that the fundamental principles of Yoga which were laid down thousands of years ago are still the most relevant in this highly competitive world where everyone is looking for quick wins and long terms solutions.

---

19 https://blog.spjain.org/articles/yoga-the-spiritual-side-of-life

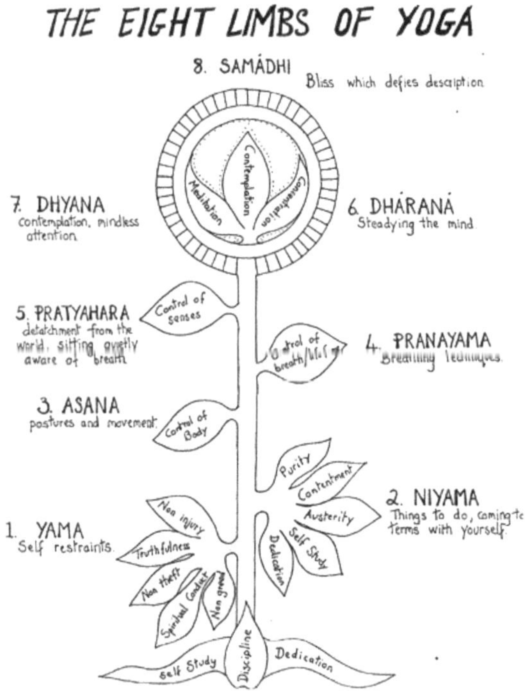

There are eight limbs of Yoga as per Maharishi Patanjali who is considered as the father of Yoga since he had formally documented the principles thousands of years back in his book – Yoga Sutra. Maharishi focused on eight important facets of living life in the perfect way. I will try to establish a parallelism between a few of these sutras to corporate life

1) **Yama** – Self restraints

   I certainly feel this principle is the foundation for living the best in corporate life. If we practice following – Yama principle in the corporate world, we certainly can avoid clashes of egos; we can maintain our composure, we can certainly be truthful in our conducts while serving our customer to the fullest. This principle helps to build discipline in our actions and work in the corporate world.

2) **Niyama** – Things to do, and coming to terms with yourself.

   This principle helps us to follow the rules and ethics in the corporate world; it helps us to come to terms with ourself by following the policy, procedures and compliance laid out by the company within the corporate world. This principle also helps us to bring focus and dedication to our work for fulfilling the requirements of our clients/customers.

3) **Asana** – Control on the body- Postures and movements

   In the corporate world there is so much of stress and pressure to meet the aspiration of individuals, team, leaders, and customers and even personal, at times we feel drained out and completely torn apart. This principle helps us to bring the focus back on the good health of our physical body. As machine requires regular maintenance and down-time, so is the case with our body. We need to rest our body at least 7-8 hours daily to be prepared for the next day's work with full enthusiasm and zeal. Asana principle helps to rejuvenate our body, mind and soul.

4) **Pranayama** – Breathing techniques

   This principle helps to have better control over breathing patterns, and by controlling our breathing patterns, we can control our body and minds. Breathing is the most fundamental part of life which we usually take for granted, but it is the most important for survival. This principle helps us bring the focus back on fundamentals in the corporate world.

5) **Pratyahara** – Control of the senses

   This principle basically teaches taking back control of situations in the corporate world when it is turning worse, driving and maneuvering through a hard time and trying to bring back normalcy in handling crisis at customer end. This principle helps in bringing back the focus of the company on success for all.

6) **Dharana** – Steadying the mind

   It is said that a steady mind can only make wise decisions which help in bringing long terms success for organization and individuals. This principle helps in steadying the mind during critical situations of decision making in corporate life. It is most important for Top organizational leaders while making decisions on the vision, mission and long-term strategy for the company.

7) **Dhyana** – contemplation and meditation

   This principle helps to bring harmony within the self and organization. By practising this principle, we can easily handle conflicting situations in the teams, workgroups and organization. This also helps in managing Organizational Change management in a better and effective manner.

8) **Samadhi** – Bliss which defies description

   This principle is the highest state an organization or individual can attain in their life span. This is the highest degree of discipline (level 5 organizations). The organization becomes self-sustaining and will surely attain significant results at this state. Organizations following this principle are sure to be called "Great Organizations and pave the path for the followers to imitate them".

I believe that if we practice these fundamental principles on a regular basis in our individual life and corporate world, we can achieve wonderful results. It is the secret sauce for achieving long-lasting success. It helps in bringing harmony and alignment between individuals and organizational goals for sustained achievements

My thoughts on the importance of Yoga in this digital world got published in the Enterprise IT world as well.

Importance of Yoga in this Digital World [20]

In today's world, CIOs and CISOs who lead IT transformations and IT security across the organizations are the key drivers for bringing change in the businesses, and they have a greater role to play in the organization. There is a famous saying that "Healthy Mind stays in Healthy Body". Also, there is a saying in IT corridors as well: if your systems are to be safe and secure, please patch and upgrade your systems on a regular basis. So here it goes: Physical Human body – **"like an IT Hardware which certainly needs regularly planned down-time for patching and maintenance work" – it similarly needs regular downtime in the form of sound sleep and patching in the form of work-out – Yoga Asana**.

IT Hardware certainly requires **software for running it effectively**, so is the human body (like hardware) that **requires MIND, which is the working software for driving the body**. As software is an equally important component of the IT landscape, so is Mind: it is the driving force for the human body.

On similar lines: we need electricity/current/power for keeping our IT systems up and running, in our case: our breath is the running current/electricity which fuels up our body and mind. Without breath, body and mind are dead and of no use, so breath plays a pivotal role in keeping us all alive.

So for CIO/CISO, IT systems are bread and butter for running their business, and so is with humans: you need to have a healthy body, mind and breath for keeping you up and running and YOGA helps us bringing the harmony between all these components.

YOGA in IT terms can be defined as a firewall which helps protect our HUMAN SYSTEM.

---

20 https://www.enterpriseitworld.com/importance-of-yoga-way-to-lead-healthy-life/

Yoga as a word has a root origin from Yug – "Union" which means bringing harmony between different systems.

In technical terms, Yoga has different components such as "**Asanas, Pranayama and Dhayana**" for taking care of each component of the Human system. Asanas are for keeping physical body fit and running; Pranayama is for regulating the breath and maintaining the flow of energy in the human body and Dhayana is for taming the mind which is the most important component of the human body like an IT Software.

So, today's CIO and CISO are examples of perfect YOGIs which balances out all IT systems- keep them up and running, help business in bringing transformation by keeping them SECURE.

Also, as perfect YOGIs: they are all singularly focused on bringing harmony to their own lives and IT system landscape as well.

Let all CIOs and CISOs take this pledge for ensuring their physical and mental well-being by sparing 30 mins time on a daily basis for themselves. It does wonders in a long time.

YOGA for healthy living of CIOs and CISOs and healthy well-being of our IT systems.

Importance of Yoga Principles in the start-up ecosystem

The start-up ecosystem is always agile and always tests the entrepreneurship skills of Young India. Startups take risks to get high rewards. Basic principles of Yoga can be followed in the start-up ecosystem for effective results.

In the start-up environment, there are no defined responsibilities; individuals take end to end responsibilities and feel more empowered as there is a sense of belongingness as they are the creators of the organization.

Yama and Niyama principles which heavily focus on self-discipline are very much required in the start-up ecosystem to keep the organization focused on the growth based on the strategy of the set-up. Moreover, start-ups have limited resources; hence they need to follow Yama and Niyama principle to be prudent in their approach to achieve best from the limited resources.

Principles of Pratyahara and Dharana helps in bringing complete focus on the organizational goals and working fundamentally to achieve those goals. It helps you filter out any distractions in the path, to ensure the success of the start-up eco-system.

SOCIETY LEVEL

Bringing transformational changes at the society level

Societies are the reflections of human growth and prosperity in the true sense. Today as we measure the growth of countries in terms of their GDPs figures and overall living standards of people around the world, it seems that human beings have reached the stage where it seems nothing is impossible in this age. We have built glorious civilizations by multiple discoveries and accomplishments. Global Technologies and inventions have created the world which once used to only exist in our imaginations. The world has become truly a global village, where each day we make impossible into possible. However, with this development, we have created lots of chaos, and we have forgotten our purpose for existence due to being too engrossed into material gains. There are rising cases of broken families, unhappiness, depression, stress, suicides. These need to be addressed by being focused on the basics of life- finding harmonies in all our actions, thoughts and energies.

Transformation at the society level can be experienced by bringing transformation at an individual level and spreading the awareness of "SELF" across all the individuals in the society. We need to start asking ourselves the true purpose of existence to uplift everyone from body consciousness to SOUL consciousness. Meditation is the most powerful way to experience this SOUL consciousness. If we can ensure all individuals in the society start practising meditation on a regular basis, we can certainly observe transformational changes on this planet Earth.

What is Meditation

English word Meditation is derived from Old French meditation, in turn from Latin meditation from a verb meditate, meaning "to think, contemplate, devise, ponder".

During one of the advance knowledge and meditation session with Brahma Kumaris. I got to understand the definition of Raja Yoga meditation

Definition of Rajyoga meditation is – Forget your body and all bodily relations, possessions and consider yourself as a point of light (Soul) sitting in between your eyebrows and remember GOD- the supreme light. This is called Rajyoga meditation

As part of traditional Raj-Yoga meditation, it comprises of 3 processes:

- **Contemplation**: focus on the thoughts running into your mind. Accept all the thoughts generated in your mind, don't resist or engage with them. Just accept them as they are. Don't label them good or bad. Consider them like clouds moving in the sky, which is not impacting sky in anyways. Same is with you; these thoughts are not impacting you in anyways. You are just observing them as a 3rd person from outside without any feelings of attachment or detachment. You are not getting impacted with them. You are not the thoughts; they are different than you.
- **Concentration**: After some period, when thoughts in your mind are getting settled, just concentrate on your forehead chakra (3rd eye chakra) as a point of light. Concentrate on the thought that I am a "Peaceful, lovable and Powerful Soul" – Owner of this body and remain in this thought for some time

- **Realization**: With continuous and daily practice, you will start having the realization of "who am I" and transformation would start happening from you being a "body consciousness" to "soul consciousness". You will start observing the difference in your nature and you having those seven innate qualities of SOUL.
- **Once you are a regular practitioner, you can start having this realization at every moment as SOUL Consciousness with your eyes even open, and you can keep meditating on this thought while performing any action of your life and subsequently this thought becomes ever-pervasive in you.**
- **In the starting of your meditation journey, you can start pondering on this thought for 30 secs to 3 mins on a daily basis once you wake up first thing in the morning and the last thing before going to bed in the night.**

8 Powers of Rajyoga

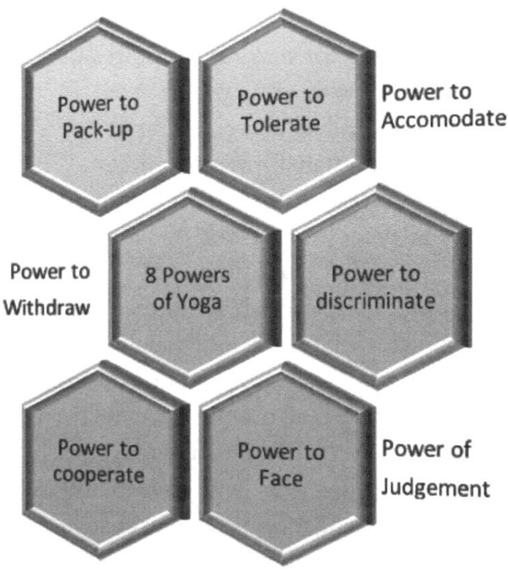

During one of the sessions with Brahma Kumari, I got to know about these eight powers of Yoga, and I agree with it. With regular practice of Rajyoga, it has tremendous positive impacts on body, mind, thoughts and actions. It helps you to align all your life energy in the right direction and helps in bringing transformational changes in individuals' life. Let's talk about a few of the powers that yoga helps you to create within you.

- **Power to Tolerate**: it improves the ability to respond to external and internal events positively and yet not be affected by them. Let's understand it with a story: once in a temple's sanctum, there was a God's Idol made of Stone, who was being asked questions by another Stone that made up the temple's floor way. The floor stone asked the idol stone, "why do people bow down in front of you, whereas the same people pass over us and don't even acknowledge putting their feet on us, although both of us come from the same stone mines? Why is there so much difference in both our treatments?" To this, the idol stone very politely replied to the footstone, "My dear friend, both of us are picked by the artists at the same time for making sculptures out it, but when they started with you, you resisted to the constant hammering, nailing and chiseling and you broke down in between the transformation process. When he picked me up, I tolerated those hard hammering, nailing and chiseling process, so I got transformed into an idol. Since you broke apart into pieces, hence you were made footstone. I was carved out in the God Idol, so life is always like that for all individuals. It provides ample opportunities to all of us to be footstone or a God's Idol, the choice is all ours, to have the perseverance and tolerance to be crafted into a masterpiece by the master who is directing this world. Certainly, with regular practice of Yoga, it brings innate changes in the overall tolerance level of individuals and he/she can face life more positively and head-on without breaking down in front of challenges offered by life.

- **Power to accommodate**: Yoga improves the ability to expand and accept the presence, ideas and desires of others. The biggest problem of the world is this statement: "I am correct, and you are wrong". With changing times, people have forgotten the art of accommodating to the changes. We have become more like individuals: "My way or the highway", resulting in conflicts most of the times. Power of accommodation is the biggest asset for the individual; it is only possible when you have compassion for others to understand them and accept them with an open heart without seeking any of the intention/favours in the relationship. This is the key to the success of any of the relationships in the world.

- **Power to discriminate**: Most of the time, this power gets misinterpreted by many in a different manner: when we say power to discriminate, it means that ability to discern the subtle and separate what is true from what is false. Nowadays, there is so much of information, data and noise all around, with multitudes of choices, it has become tough for individuals to pick what is truth in this overall maze. Moreover, whenever we reach higher up in personal or professional life, this is the most important quality a person needs to possess to be successful. He/she needs to filter out the signal from the noise. Since all of us are only blessed to have 24 hours in a day and volume of information increasing by leaps and bounds, there are lots of decisions to be made daily, and here the power of discrimination comes handy and helps you to be successful in your life.

- **Power of judgement**: This power means the ability to assess the quality of choices, decisions and actions in yourself and others. It is often said that life is all about the choices you make and the decisions you make. Your choices and decisions of today are going to chalk out your future course of action. For taking any kind of decisions, you need to have a steady mind which helps in making the rational or correct decision based on the available circumstances. I got to know about **HALT** during one of the leadership training sessions. We can use **HALT methods** for effective decision or rather never make any major decisions during these circumstances

- H: Hungry or Hurry: whenever you are hungry or in a hurry, never try to make any critical decision because of those circumstances or that times, we don't consider the overall impact of the decision which we make in haste or during hunger.
- A: Angry: A lot have been said about anger and anger management. Any decision made during that time frame needs to be avoided since we lose our control of making rational choices when we are angry.
- L: Lonely: when you feel lonely, you need to avoid making any critical decision making of life, since a lonely state of mind will be always devoid you of critical thinking and correct decision-making process
- T: Tired: whenever you are deeply tired and about to sleep, never take any crucial decisions of life as we often miss out minute details and potential impact of choices and decisions.

- **Power to face**: This power means the ability to face tough times with ease and smile in life or confront and resolve external and internal obstacles, tests and challenges happily. It is rightly said, the wisdom of the man is tested in unfavourable times since in good times, it is always smooth sailing for all of us. The wise men are the ones who remain unperturbed by lows and highs of life.

- **Power to cooperate:** This power means the ability to give attention, time, experience and wisdom in the service of others and to work alongside them unintentionally. We all will always want to find: "WHAT IS IT FOR ME" for whatever tasks which we perform. Doing a selfless service is called SEVA for self, society and mankind at large.

  We have seen multitudes of examples in corporates, societies and nations at large; all are bonded by common goals and purpose. All collaborate and cooperate for a purpose without looking into: "What is in it for me". Power to cooperate helps to bring that unity among mankind and societies at large. Cooperation is the only way by which we all can survive all odds of life. We need to work as a team to achieve success in life.

  Also, if deeply observe an individual – its body, mind, thoughts, energy and actions need to be aligned in a single direction for achieving success. Power of cooperation certainly does wonders to all.

Storytime – To Explain The Power Of Cooperation

In ancient times, there were Angels and Devils (Suras and Asuras). One day, they went to Brahma – Creator of this world, asking who was superior among Suras and Asuras. Devils were adamant and forcing him to declare them as superior. Lord Brahma told both, lets us decide this by completing a challenge. He called both Suras and Asuras gave them the task of eating the food without folding their hands. Suras and Asuras started thinking about it. To prove their superiority, Asuras started. First, they all tried, but they were not able to eat food without folding their hands, they started throwing the food upwards for grasping it, but most of the food got wasted, and they all remained hungry.

When the turn of Suras came, they used a trick; they got paired up by facing one another – as a pair, they picked up food and started feeding each other, with this idea they were able to settle down their hunger and proved to be better than Asuras.

- **Power to withdraw:** This power is the ability to step back and disengage from the world around you. This is the most important and relevant in today's world, which is full of turbulence and noise all around. Let's take an example of a tortoise; whenever it senses any turbulence around itself, it withdraws and takes back all its limbs inside the thick shell which protects it from any kind of adversities around it. This power gives you the inner strength to withdraw yourself from the outside world and help you to have a connection established within you. When an individual has a connection established within himself – say Soul or SELF or Atman, he usually attains the state of bliss and always stays happy in any circumstances.

  It requires a tremendous amount of discipline to have self-control or withdrawals from the outer world which we call as Samsara or Maya since the mind is always running in past or future and to have it stabilize in the present by withdrawing it with worldly affairs require regular practice and a deep sense of discipline.

- **Power to Pack-up:** This power refers to the ability to bring things to an end and to stop wasteful thinking. Most of the time, all human beings get so engrossed in the deep sense of ownership and engagement that they don't have any end to it. The individual keeps on doing whatever they enjoy doing, whether it is resulting in any benefit or not, is considered secondary. At times, this results in a waste of energy and resources. The wise person always knows when to put a full-stop to work/ task or assignment he or she is working on.

In organizations, most of the times, individuals or teams work with their motives, which results in reduced productivity for the organization at large. Hence, it is the responsibility of leaders to understand when to pack-up in these kinds of circumstance to avoid productivity losses.

Transformation at Different countries or Government levels

Transformation around the world is only possible when we start imbibing the fundamental of Yoga principles on a daily basis. Taking time out for Practicing Yoga and meditation on a daily basis helps us realize this question: WHO AM I? and "what is the true purpose of life."

Once you start seeing life as a theatre with a well-written script by LORD ALMIGHTY, You and me as just actors coming and performing our roles assigned to us and enjoying the role without questioning or judging it, then the world starts looking up to you in perfect order, and this chaos looks to you as an ideal symphony for admiring and enjoying.

So, STOP JUDGING AND KEEP EXPERIENCING the life

I want to conclude my book with a short and impactful story for some food for thought

Don't be a Gamma in the land of Lama

I was attending my regular meditation course and got a chance to interact with EV Swaminathan sir. He started his session by sharing this wonderful short story with all the attendees. Here goes the story:

Long long ago, there were two disciples of a Great Guru in the land of Siachen. Names of those disciples were – Lama and Gamma. Lama used to always be very happy and cheerful in life in whatever situations of life around him. He used to enjoy every moment and was full of life. On the other hand, Gamma used to be always sad, gloomy, thinking and worrisome. He would always find faults in whatever kind of situations he was in. The Guru or Saint daily used to give knowledge discourse to both students and used to have Yoga sessions to improve the overall quality of life for these folks. Lama, as usual, used to be very happy after attending all those sessions, and Gamma would always crib about these sessions.

One day Guru came to know about it, and decided not to take any session but instead gave both of them a task. Guruji brought baskets of flowers and divided among them and told it both of them that they need to go out in the nearby village and distribute these flowers to whosoever they find happy, cheerful. Once all the flowers in their baskets are allocated, they need to return to the ashram as early as possible. This was like a task or challenge given to both. Lama took the basket of flowers and went in one direction, and Gamma took it and went in another direction. Within 30 mins time, Lama returned, smiling with an empty basket and told his Guru, it was such an easy task for him. Guruji appreciated and asked him to wait for his other colleague and friend Gamma to return. Hours passed by. It became afternoon from the morning, and then soon it was evening, and the sun was about to set, but Gamma still hadn't come back. Another hour passed by, it was now dark all around, and both Guruji and Lama started worrying about the well-being of Gamma and wondering why Gamma still didn't come back. Suddenly to their surprise, they saw Gamma coming back from the dark, full of sweat and frustration on his face with the basket full of flowers on his head. Guruji asked Gamma: "What happened my child? You looked so tired and frustrated. Was everything alright?"

To this question, Gamma replied, "Guruji, you gave me such a tough task of distributing these flowers to whosoever I met in my way who was happy and smiling, but in these days you know, there is no-one happy and smiling. How could I had given these flowers to anyone who was not smiling as you mentioned me to give this to only smiling face only."

To this, Guruji looked at Lama and asked him: "How come you were able to complete this task within 20-30 mins and came back so early, and Gamma found this so difficult and tiring?"

Lama replied with utter surprise and said, "Whenever I had met anyone, I met with a smile on my face and was always greeted back by the person on another side with a smile, and when I saw them smiling back to me, I gave them these flowers and hence was able to get this task done within 20-30 mins time."

Gamma understood the game of life: if you expect back smile from others, you need to give them at least the same thing in return. He remembered whenever he was doing this task; he had a tiring and troubled and grim face with which he looked at others and others when they looked back to him reciprocated in the same manner.

To this, Guruji replied to both his disciples with a beautiful answer: "Life is like a mirror, whatever you will give it to it, and you will find it returning to you."

When Swami sir finished his story, I understood, we all behave immaturely like Gammas in our whole life which is always full of love, peace, bliss and affection. It is important to change the attitude towards life to observe the change within you and around the world. All of us are born as lamas of the world – always being happy if you observe a newly born baby, he doesn't have any understanding of the outer world, but he is always smiling and greeting you – known or unknown person, but as we grow up, we get layers created around us, we forget the most pleasant gift of our life – the smile, and slowly we get ourselves transformed from peaceful Lama to Gamma. True knowledge of self helps us to be lama again in life.

Pearls of wisdom from various Gurus/Yogis/Mystics for peaceful and contented living

- I am the creator of my own thoughts; there should be complete awareness in me about my thoughts
- Like physical immunity is built by Yoga asanas, mental immunity is created by meditation
- There is nothing called competition in life; everyone has their own journey to travel
- What I – Eat, Watch, Listen and Read – is who I become over a period
- Take time to Mediate. Meditate daily at least for 30 mins, to begin with
- Our thoughts create our world
- De-clutter your physical space
- Start making a habit of scribing or writing a journal, diary or notes for the day
- Reduce consuming toxic information
- Go Minimalist
- Earn with Passion, spend with compassion
- Talk it out
- Put others first
- Practice Mindfulness in every task performed by you
- Life is the most difficult exam; many people fail because they try to copy others, not realizing that everyone has got a different question paper
- Everyone's life is a different journey with their own challenges to overcome and successes to celebrate
- Silence is the most powerful dimension of life – experience it
- My responsibilities are limitless, and My needs are limited. This thought gives us empowerment

- The present moment is inevitable. The way it is – is the way it is
- This body and this mind are just the gatherings; this is not me.
- Death is the truth; accept this thought, and you will get liberated from this fear forever.

PART 5

SMILING FACES AFTER YOGA AND MEDITATION PRACTICE

> Meditate, do Satsang, read knowledge sheets. By doing that you are helping others who have a hard time.
>
> – GURU DEV SRI SRI

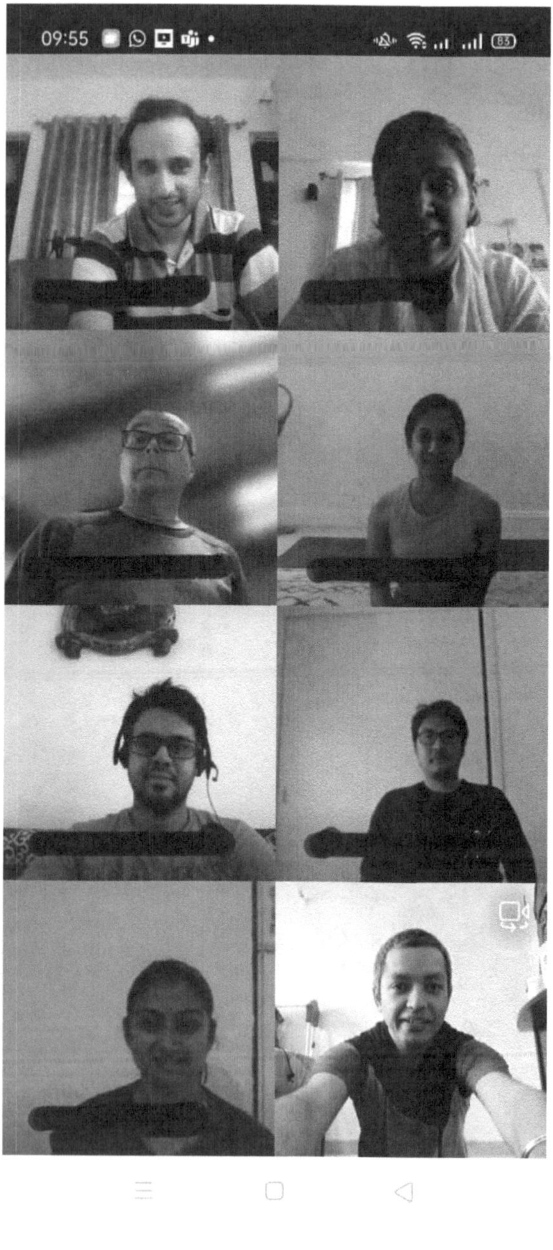

Cyber Frat
JEGADEESWARAN

References:

https://thewellnessenterprise.com/emoto/

Types of thoughts : https://www.speakingtree.in/blog/4-types-of-thoughts-that-impacts-everyone

Steve Jobs last words : https://www.nytimes.com/2011/10/30/opinion/mona-simpsons-eulogy-for-steve-jobs.html?pagewanted=all